STONE, STEEL & SPIRIT

INDIANA STATE MUSEUM

emmis books
1700 Madison Road Cincinnati, Ohio 45206 www.emmisbooks.com

Indiana State

MUSEUM

©Copyright 2004

Indiana State Museum

Indianapolis, Indiana

All rights reserved under

International and

Pan-American Copyright

Conventions

Published in the United States by

Emmis Books, Inc. Cincinnati, OH

ISBN 1-57860-162-2

Library of Congress Control Number: 2004106415

DEDICATION

GOVERNOR FRANK O'BANNON *shared a deep philosophical belief that providing an appropriate venue to gather and to celebrate Indiana's culture and heritage would serve as a source of pride in our past and help build a bridge to the future. The vision became reality as a direct result of his commitment to principle, his strength of will and his powers of friendly persuasion. He provided the Indiana State Museum project team with the resources to procure the stone and the steel and challenged us to create a place that would capture the essence of the Hoosier spirit...perhaps best personified by Governor O'Bannon himself. It was his vision and unwavering commitment that inspired the project team to explore new and courageous concepts, both in the building architecture and the exhibit design. Every person who had a hand in the making of the Indiana State Museum recognizes that they were given an unparalleled opportunity to make a lasting mark on the Hoosier landscape. It was a privilege to be entrusted to lead this project.*

STONE, STEEL AND SPIRIT
is dedicated to the memory of Governor Frank O'Bannon.
—SUSAN WILLIAMS

On the afternoon of April 4, 2001 Governor Frank O'Bannon and First Lady Judy O'Bannon signed the last steel beam during the Museum's "topping out," the celebration that accompanies the placing of the last beam in any major construction project.

*The Indiana State Museum
seen from the south lawn.*

Contents

PREFACE

History is, at heart, a dialogue between the present and the past, in hope of the future. Architecture is the most visible history: It embodies the past as prelude, then turns to address the future, where it will live. Museums, those buildings most focused on the past, are also the most determined votes of confidence in the future. Museums are built hopefully, that our descendants will celebrate what has come before them. And museums are built knowingly: We know our descendants must know the past to know themselves.

Despite the fact that architecture is the most public art form, it often needs the most explanation. Buildings by their sheer size announce themselves to the world with such tangible presence that words seem superfluous, air upon stone. Yet eventually the excitement of newness evaporates and even the finest new architecture becomes unseen backdrop, a piece of mute sculpture, its stories forgotten, its image dulled by exposure.

This book hopes to preserve the spirit that built the Indiana State Museum, to remember its stories, to brighten its image in words the future can most readily grasp. This is not a definitive history of the building or the institution, although such a text would be a valuable addition to Indiana literature. It is, rather, an informed celebration. It celebrates a marvelous architectural achievement and a design built of boldness and innovation. Equally, it celebrates the success of that design in the larger realm of public ideals and civic meaning. The Museum has brought a new vocabulary to Indiana's public architecture, a new expectation that public design speak to the people and for the people of Indiana, and find in Indiana the foundation of its vision. In its first year, the Museum spoke that message to thousands of visitors. We trust this grand design will continue to speak clearly and forcefully until the day, many years in the future, when new concepts of museums and new ways of presenting the story of Indiana will require a new design built on the same foundations.

Above: Aerial view to the north showing the triptych of museums: (l-r) NCAA Hall of Champions, Indiana State Museum and Eiteljorg Museum.

Opposite: Ratio Architect's original drawing of the south façade.

BUILDING THE INDIANA STATE MUSEUM

The sky was bluer than it had been in years, a glorious blue, a first blue. So it felt the morning of May 22, 2002, opening day at the new Indiana State Museum in White River State Park. The sky was glorious and the sun was shining so brightly that most everyone sitting on the ceremonial platform in front of the main museum entrance was obliged to wear sunglasses, a rarity for people accustomed to the glare of public life. Somehow this day was brighter than that. At the foot of the grand limestone wall that forms the Museum's south face, a long line of yellow school buses delivered a river of 600 children drawn from across the state. Hundreds more Hoosiers stood waiting across the expanse of green lawn in front of the museum.

As the crowd watched expectantly, Museum architect Bill Browne handed the key to the building to his client, Susan Williams, director of the Indiana State Office Building Commission, who had overseen the project for the previous four years. She, in turn, delivered the key to her tenant (and boss), Gov. Frank O'Bannon, who accepted it on behalf of his boss – the people of Indiana.

After a fitting number of proud pronouncements and appreciations, these three, along with First Lady Judy O'Bannon and a line of other dignitaries, stepped to the long, ceremonial ribbon stretched before the Museum doors. Taking their cue from Gov. O'Bannon, the dignitaries scissored the ribbon simultaneously: The new Indiana State Museum was officially open.

First through the doors were the people. Not the official people, not the movers and shakers and those who steered the state, but the children, grandchildren and great-grandchildren of those whose hearts and hands had built this state. All those who had quarried and carved, welded, drilled, painted and polished, planted and harvested, written and spoken the heritage collected inside those just-opened doors. The Gov. and Mrs. O'Bannon stood outside as the crowd streamed past, smiling and greeting them as they entered their building.

As Williams remembered the day, the O'Bannons were so busy welcoming the citizens of Indiana that they never had the chance to make the 100-foot walk from the main entrance on the south to the broad terrace on the Museum's north side where cake and punch were being served. It really didn't matter. The sunlight and the smiles beneath that grand south wall were enough that day.

That day, opening day of the first Indiana State Museum designed specifically as a museum, had been a very long time coming. This building had been born in spirit in the 19th century and erected in stone and steel in the 21st, requiring an instant to imagine and the span of three centuries to realize.

Should we start the story in 1837 when the newly appointed State Geologist first gathered a shelf of mineral samples? Or should we consider the question more tangibly and start with the groundbreaking on this site on August 30, 1999? Perhaps it makes more sense to turn back to the late 1880s when the rudimentary museum collections were first given their own room in the newly constructed Statehouse. Should we even consider that assemblage of rocks and stuffed ani-

Opposite Page Left: Cutting the ribbon to welcome the citizens of Indiana to their new Museum. (l-r) Susan Williams, First Lady Judy O'Bannon, Dalibor Plecan, Gov. Frank O'Bannon, and Sadeeq Danbala. The two students won a statewide essay competition.

Opposite Page Right: Indiana State Office Building Commission Executive Director Susan Williams hands the ceremonial key to the Indiana State Museum to Gov. Frank O'Bannon, May 22, 2002.

This Page: Opening ceremonies on the south lawn of the new Indiana State Museum.

*Gala reception on the eve of
the Museum's grand opening,
May 21, 2002.*

mals a museum collection? Maybe we should start in the late 1940s when state government first considered and then rejected the idea of a separate facility to house the collection. Or maybe should we start a decade later when the idea received its first serious public support? All such questions only beg others and all demand some fundamental definitions.

Was the collection itself, with whatever gaps and omissions, the Museum? Or was the Museum the idea of telling

they did draw human ore, and brought thousands of immigrants to Indiana, sometimes drawn by the hope of work, some passing through on their way to other opportunities. Those that stayed became deeply rooted. And once rooted, the people embraced Indiana tightly. Generations of Hoosiers have come to regard the hills and valleys, forests, shores, plains and rivers of their state as illustrating their innermost spirit, seen equally in the cool sparkle of moonlight

Left to Right:
Sunny Autumn Day c. 1947
Frank V. Dudley (1868-1957)

Early Spring c. 1930
Curry Bohm (1894-1971)

Pastoral 1886
T.C. Steele (1847-1926)

Indiana's story through artifacts? And where does that larger story begin?

Latitude and longitude can tell us where Indiana starts and stops but tell us nothing of Hoosier spirit. But geography and its sister geology can help us. Each state has been dealt its own geological hand with whatever natural resources and attractions that might include, whether rich topsoil or buried stone, hushed forests or roaring rivers – or, in the case of Indiana, relatively quiet rivers that obliged the state to look elsewhere for transportation. Sometimes those resources have played enormous roles in the culture of state. Quite apart from its impact on the economic health of Indiana, the state's limestone has provided common character to nearly every major public edifice in the state's nearly 200 year history. It was almost inconceivable that the new Museum would present itself as anything but a celebration of limestone.

Other resources have made significant contributions to the state's history and culture. The natural gas flames that once fired the state's thriving glass industry are now cold, but they left a legacy of craftsmanship that can still be felt. The steel mills of "The Region" of northwestern Indiana may not have drawn iron ore from the Hoosier hills, but

on the Wabash and the blazing golds and reds of a Brown County autumn. It may be debated whether such images are a cause or an effect of the so-called Hoosier School of painting from the late 1800s and early 1900s, but the fact remains that the greatest artistic movement yet produced by the state focused on landscape painting. To this day, that collection remains one of the most tenaciously popular attractions of the Museum, the landscape embraced as a metaphoric self-portrait of the state.

Ask architect Bill Browne what makes a Hoosier and he'll just shrug and ask if you've got a day or two to chat. When he began to consider the design of the new Indiana State Museum, Browne and his firm, Ratio Architects, spent weeks surveying the terrain of the Hoosier soul so that their design might stand at just the right point of the state's inner map.

Conservativism, Browne says, is the bedrock of that inner geography. Here in the "heart of the heart of the country," to borrow a phrase from author William Gass, Indiana is far from the cutting edges of either coast and, truth be told, often dismissive of their fluttering whims of cultural fashion. Hoosiers prefer the stability of knowing where they come from and where they're going – slowly, at that.

LIMESTONE

The life and history of Indiana has been carved in limestone. For more than a century, limestone has been the signature material for all major state-sponsored and many privately-funded buildings. It is the state's most distinctive export. The citizens of the state conceive of it as an institution because, in so many instances, its identity is seen tangibly in its built institutions, its bedrock limestone made into its schools and courthouses, hospitals and houses of worship. Limestone is the state's foundation and its home. As such, its use as the predominant surface for the Indiana State Museum was not a matter of aesthetic preference; it was an issue of identity.

First quarried near Stinesville in 1827, limestone served a mostly local market until the Chicago fire of 1871, when the durability of limestone structures multiplied demand during the city's rebuilding. Architectural aesthetics then multiplied it even more. For nearly a century, from the end of the Civil War until the end of World War II, American institutional architecture was dominated by a narrow range of historical revival styles that favored easily workable, light-colored stone for structural, cladding and decorative uses. Indiana limestone was the answer.

Even the Great Depression did not immediately slow demand. The late 1920s and early '30s were actually boom years for Indiana limestone. In 1929, the state quarried twelve million cubic feet for the nation's architects, almost all of it used in large-scale projects for institutional or governmental clients.

That may be the most salient factor in understanding the meaning of Indiana limestone. Although limestone is inextricably from a vision of Hoosier life, it is equally or more central to America's image of itself as a set of institutions – as universities, museums and churches, as capitols and corporations, as almost any edifice containing the things that we value.

A very partial list of national structures built with Indiana limestone includes the capitol buildings of 35 states, the Empire State Building, the Pentagon, the National Cathedral, the U.S. Department of Commerce, George W. Vanderbilt's Biltmore, the Chicago Tribune Tower, the Ronald Reagan Building in D.C., the U.S. Holocaust Memorial Museum in Washington, D.C., 101 Federal Street building in Boston, Massachusetts – and the Indiana State Museum.

The great south wall of the Museum, truly its signature public image, is a monumental assembly of over 6,000 rough-faced limestone blocks, punctuated by a main entrance executed in gleaming stainless steel and glass. Like every other major design element in the Museum this wall has its story, actually stories – some literal and practical, others metaphoric and aesthetic.

Technically, the pattern of the wall is called random ashlar, composed of interlocking rectangular stones of varying sizes. Random ashlar has been an architectural motif for thousands of years, and bespeaks an almost proto-historic construction. It can be used with either dressed or rough stone, although as far as the design team at Ratio Architects could determine, it had never been attempted at this mammoth scale – nearly 300 ft. by 65 ft. This wall had to be invented, so to speak. During visits to southern Indiana limestone quarries, Ratio's Bill Browne learned about "roughbacks," the rough-textured slabs left like bread heels from a loaf when large limestone blocks are trimmed for architectural application. Although roughbacks can be quite sizable, perhaps several feet square, they are normally ground for gravel. Browne's team seized on the idea of using these stones at their available size, and assembling them on this unprecedented scale for the Museum's main face. To do so required the cumulative roughback output of the entire Indiana limestone industry for a year, assembled and cut at the quarries of the Evans Limestone Company.

Almost from the outset, the design team from Ratio Architects had envisioned the Museum's south face wall metaphorically as a "garden wall," a wall to border the vast landscaping of the White River State Park. Yet at this monumental scale the garden wall is also a fortress wall, signifying the historic position of Indiana as the boundary between the American wilderness and its East Coast civilization. The wilderness had been surveyed and impressed with the rectangular plan of civilization, but it maintained a roughhewn character that all the geometry in the world could not smooth over. This wall is the rough, closed, conservative face of pioneer Indiana.

Standing beneath the massive wall, we look up and see…the cragged but multileveled walls of well-worked quarries – perhaps the pieced puzzle of our state's counties or even the larger map of the nation west of Indiana. The visual metaphors are available but none is enforced, leaving the south wall forever open to the viewer's musings. The great assembly of individual pieces, each unique yet united as a whole, offers us whatever we are capable of seeing, Indiana's self-portrait in stone.

Above: Indiana limestone fills the air in the fabrication facility of the Bybee Limestone Company. Bybee craftsmen carved many of the icons for the Museum's 92 County Walk. For well over a century Hoosiers have worked the stone for some of America's most significant landmarks, including the Pentagon, the Empire State Building and the National Cathedral in Washington, D.C. Constructing the Indiana State Museum required nearly five million pounds of limestone quarried throughout the state's limestone region. The Evans Limestone Company of Bedford managed all aspects of this herculean effort, quarrying, cutting, dressing, fabricating and transporting the stone to the construction site.

Far Left: The Empire State Building.

Left: The National Cathedral in Washington, D.C.

The majestic vision of City Beautiful urban planning is seen in this procession of grand public spaces and structures through the heart of Indianapolis: University Square *in the foreground to Indiana World War Memorial, Obelisk Square, American Legion Mall and the Indianapolis-Marion County Public Library.*

On the other hand, Browne is quick to add, Hoosiers can be a quirky lot. As much as they prize the stability and traditions, they take equal pride in being the pivot point of so much national coming and going, of being the "Crossroads of America," as the state motto has proclaimed since 1937. Stability and mobility make a strange cultural mix, giving Hoosiers a certain contrariness of spirit that serves the state well when the rest of the country seems to be strolling blithely off a cliff – and not so well when fast changing times demand swift response.

If they are a paradox to themselves, Hoosiers are even more a moving target to outsiders. Depending on how you look at it, Indiana can be cast as the farthest extension of Southern culture by Northerners looking down, or as the first Yankee state by Southerners looking north. It may be seen as the last outpost of the gentrified East by Westerners looking back; or, to citified Easterners, as the first step past the invisible wall that separates the cultured from the unkempt.

Assaulted by such perceptions on all sides, is it any wonder that Indiana remains determinedly in its own time zone? Others may not quite know where or when to find the state, but it has always been right here. "It was this dichotomy that we saw at the root of the Hoosier psyche, and it was this dichotomy that we wanted to explore in the design of the State Museum," Browne said.

If defining Hoosier character was an elusive proposition riddled with contradictions, it was no less problematic to define the modern museum.

Historically, the architectural paradigm of a museum was fairly straightforward, perhaps even obvious in the understood context of civic design. Museums, it was assumed, were noble institutions deserving noble architectural form. That

Historically, the architectural paradigm of a museum was fairly straightforward, perhaps even obvious in the understood context of civic design.

generally meant a grand, even bombastic edifice adhering to classical design precepts and materials. It meant stone and symmetry and a scale appropriate in ancient Greece or Rome, or some imperial European capital – or their Hollywood reincarnations.

But back home again in Indiana?

There were many who would have welcomed a neo-classical approach, or at least a post-modern rendition. Much of their enthusiasm stemmed from the still warm admiration for the old Museum at 202 North Alabama Street. Designed in 1908 by the Indianapolis firm of Rubush and Hunter, that grand edifice had served as the Indianapolis City Hall before becoming the Indiana State Museum in 1967. It is some comment on the evolving sense of the natures of government and cultural institutions that the same design could be thought to embody both.

Grand-style neo-classicism is the style of America's coming of age at the turn of the last century, the style of the City Beautiful movement that transformed the hearts of dozens of American cities from Babels of architectural vocabularies into unified statements of frankly imperial scale and order. In doing so, not coincidentally, the City Beautiful movement catalyzed a national demand for Indiana limestone. The last great design campaign of this national enthusiasm can be seen in the six-block parade of grand structures and spaces carved out of downtown Indianapolis to make room for the World War Memorial, Obelisk Square and American Legion Mall. This was conceived in the early 1920s, fulfilling a promise made by a political partnership of the city and the state to attract the national headquarters of the newly formed American Legion. The design also incorporates the neo-classical library to the north and the courthouse to the south. The total archi-

tectural effect is stunning to the point of inspiring. Such was its intent.

The City Beautiful was an aesthetic of power, of America's new eminence on the world stage as the rightful inheritor of European tradition. A century later, American public architecture must speak to more than European tradition. The Museum designers also knew that neo-classical symmetry lacks and indeed, might hardly accommodate, the Hoosier quirkiness seen so keenly at the state's collective soul.

Further, the modern day museum is a far more sophisticated structure than its predecessors. Conservation technology has come a very long way since the days when stuffed owls were displayed next to Civil War flags with scant concern that either might require special environmental conditions to fend off a smorgasbord of deleterious gases, bacteria and radiation. It is sometimes joked, not by conservators, that the best way to ensure the survival of any museum artifact is to keep it locked in a dark and airless box. Modern museums have also added communications concerns, incorporating a new range of media technology that must be accommodated in their architecture.

Beyond these technological challenges, the modern museum faces a profound evolution – some would say revolution – of its core mission. Where traditionally a museum elevated and ennobled its collection, today's museum invites visitors to analyze as much as admire what they see. And where once museum planners might safely assume that visitors came well prepared with shared knowledge and attitudes, they must now educate visitors to a range of perspectives, and encourage them to gaze unafraid at the image in the mirror – to see the world, and themselves, plainly and honestly.

Further complicating the architectural challenge was the

Three banners hang in the Grand Lobby illustrating the three-fold function as a museum of art, culture and science.

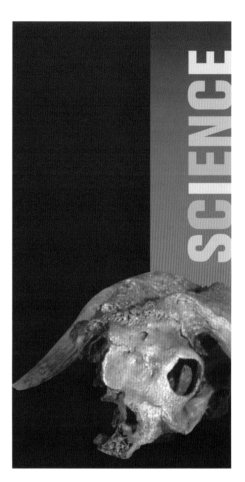

Indiana State Museum's three-fold function as a museum of art, culture and science. The Museum may be unique among state museums to the extent it devotes its energies and space more-or-less equally to each of its three functions.

Now design it all. And in a way that speaks of pride, that tells the truth and points to the future. That was the challenge that Gov. O'Bannon had given Susan Williams, and she in turn had given Ratio Architects. The fact that all were smiling broadly in that brilliant May sunshine is perhaps the best indication that the right design was found.

This is the story of that design, the story of how that future was envisioned. To understand that story and that vision fully, though, we must first look to the past.

*The first visitors enter the
Grand Lobby of the
Indiana State Museum on
opening day.*

STEEL

As visitors walk through the Indiana State Museum the strength of steel is everywhere – overhead and underfoot. In the Museum steel stands open and unclad, announcing the integrity of its structure and the honesty of its form. The exposed beams and girders create a stage set of industrial scale and muscle upon which are presented the stories of Hoosier history and spirit. The Museum is a raw-boned giant holding a cloud in its hands.

In history, in economics, in culture, steel is the great counterweight to limestone. Steel is the skeleton of Indiana's north; limestone is the bedrock of its south. Steel speaks of our urban centers and the great American waves of immigrants; limestone comes from the country and conjures memories of our earliest settlers. Steel is an assembly of elements from across an entire region of the Midwest; its presence in Indiana proves that we are truly the Crossroads of America. Limestone is pulled from the ground in one small section of the state, proving we draw our strength from this landscape. Yet there is at least this physical synergy between stone and steel: In the steel-making process, limestone is a small but necessary element, added to the furnace to draw off impurities from the molten iron.

Although limestone is rooted in the 19th century, the story of steel is a completely 20th century saga. It begins in full force in the century's first decade, from the first Inland Steel plant begun in 1901 near Hammond, to the construction of the South Shore Line in 1903, with the founding of the city of Gary by the US Steel Corporation in 1905 and the opening of its Gary Works a year later, to the creation of the Indiana Steel Harbor in 1908. From that point, the story cascades through the decades, swirling around boom and Depression, from wartime bounty to peacetime downturn, from unrivaled productivity to massive strikes. At its high point in 1979, employment in the state's steel industry reached 70,000 workers. Today at the dawn of the 21st century that figure has fallen to 33,000. But in raw tonnage Indiana still leads the nation in steel production – just as Indiana limestone is still the premier stone in the country.

Throughout the Museum, Ratio used steel both as structure and as

The steel bents spring over the top of the future limestone quarry exhibit.

symbol. Steel holds the Museum together and expresses the greatness of Indiana's industrial century, when the northwest corner of Indiana grew into "The Region," the western crucible of the great American steel industry. The romance of those times, of 50-ton ladles of molten metal pouring amid a shower of sparks into a river of steel is still part of Indiana and still felt by many.

This vision is seen most clearly in the towering half-arches of the Grand Lobby. These mammoth steel pillars were a work unto themselves, an unprecedented assignment calling forth all the skills of engineers and fabricators of Geiger & Peters, Inc. to ensure that each stress and load was precisely calculated. Like everything else in the Museum, these multi-ton structures –simply called "bents" during the building's construction – were designed with a characteristic Hoosier angle, veering up into the northwest with nothing apparently at the end to support them. Once a vast tower of steel veers off perpendicular with no support in sight, calculation down to the ounce is required to ensure its structural integrity. That is the gift and the challenge of steel – endless design opportunity and expressive potential demand calculated confidence and measured strength.

In the Grand Lobby, each of these 100-foot "bents" tapers down to rest upon a pedestal of limestone. The message of the architecture is clear: Indiana rests on its 19th century bedrock but climbs skyward on 20th century steel. As the incomplete archway testifies, the job is still half done. The future is waiting to be built.

Steel as the skeleton of architectural space: Beams and bents, railings and supports define and contain the voluminous expanse of the Museum's Grand Lobby.

LOOKING BACK

The early years of the Indiana State Museum tell an uninspiring story. The Museum, such as it was, started from scratch in 1837 with a few dozen rock samples assembled by the first state geologist, David Dale Owen of New Harmony, meant to show legislators the mineral bounty of the state. Owen was the son of Robert Owen, founder of New Harmony, and, like his father, a man of great intellectual breadth and vision, a co-founder of the United States Geological Survey and the Smithsonian Institution. In 1862, State Librarian R. Deloss Brown began filling a "cabinet of wonders," as such things were known in the 19th century, with an assortment of mineral specimens and natural curiosities he deemed worth preserving. As returning Civil War veterans began to donate guns, swords, uniforms, flags and other mementos of the war, the legislature decided it was the state's patriotic duty to set aside space in the State Library to house it all. In 1869 the General Assembly directed the state geologist to collect and preserve "examples of Indiana's geology and animal and plant life." A year later, an appropriation for $100 was passed to build and main-

tain a large display case containing stuffed specimens of the state's wildlife. The case stood in the state geologist's boardroom but eventually filled a room of its own on the east side of the old state capitol building. When the magnificent new Statehouse opened in 1888, former legislator and State Geologist James Maurice Thompson transferred the collection to a larger room on either the third or the first floor – accounts vary.

In 1919, state government awoke to the idea of conserving and preserving the Hoosier natural heritage and created the Department of Conservation, which now included the office of the State Geologist along with its collection of artifacts. By then the collection had become a haphazard smorgasbord of all things Hoosier, a sprawling testament to the museum's policy (or lack thereof) to accept nearly anything that anyone might care to donate. Eventually the light and

This Page: David Dale Owen, the first Indiana State Geologist and founder of the Museum's paleontology collection.

Opposite Page: The Museum owns more than 300,000 skeletal remains and fossils of prehistoric creatures of the Indiana region. Pictured here are (l-r) a Harlan's Musk Ox, Gumz Farm Mastodon, and a Short-Faced Bear.

Top Left: "State of the art" conservation techniques applied via vacuum cleaner in the old Museum quarters in the basement of the Statehouse.

Top Right: Indiana businessman and philanthropist Eli Lilly (1885-1977) supported many efforts to promote the study of Indiana history and archaeology.

Bottom Left: Present-day storage vaults for the Museum's fine arts collection located in the Administration Building.

Bottom Right: The Museum's natural history specimen collection on the first floor of the Administration Building.

Left and Below: The collection of the Indiana State Museum languished for decades in the basement of the Statehouse, receiving little if any conservational or curatorial care.

prominence of its space at the Statehouse proved too attractive to other state officials. As the Department of Conservation reshuffled the deck of new and existing agencies, one of the losers was the collection, which was relocated to the Statehouse basement, near the still-functioning stables.

Almost out of sight, the collection now became largely out of mind for the next 40 years. According to former Museum Director Richard Gantz, writing in *The Encyclopedia of Indianapolis*, the basement museum "languished for 45 years. Displays were arranged in no conceivable order with few labels. The most notable item was the carcass of Hoosier Jumbo, 'The Largest Hog in the World.'" Vandalism and water damage, insects and mildew assaulted the collection. Some objects simply disappeared.

A brief light was played across the problem during the

Right: The Indiana Statehouse

administration of Gov. M. Clifford Townsend (1937-41), who aired the idea of a new facility again. Gripped by the Depression, with war on the near horizon, the General Assembly had other priorities. The collection remained in its basement obscurity. After World War II, under the leadership of Gov. Ralph F. Gates (1945-49) serious discussions of a new museum facility began floating around the highest levels of political power. Philanthropist Eli Lilly liked the idea enough to offer property at the northwest corner of Ohio and Senate streets in downtown Indianapolis as the site of a new museum. The General Assembly was still unimpressed. With or without free land, the projected construction cost of $3.5 million seemed entirely too high to contemplate.

A decade later, either the political mood had evolved or public concern had sharpened, or both. In any event, in 1957 the General Assembly appointed a Museum Study Commission to survey the situation, compare it to other states, and recommend a plan of action. The Commission noted that Indiana currently spent $5,000 annually on its collections while other states spent five or ten times as much – or more. After detailing the loss of irreplaceable artifacts through decay, inattention or incompetence, the Commission concluded that "Indiana has the poorest and most inadequate State Museum in the United States" and proposed spending $3.8 million to construct a new facility. If the Commission's report was intended to sting, the General Assembly remained steadfastly numb to its barbs. The report was accepted and filed.

Today, standing before the magnificent new Museum, it is tempting to dismiss the actions – or in this case, inactions – of earlier eras as mere political shortsightedness. That would be a mistake. The decision to do almost anything in state government is – and should be – freighted with politics. Politics is not a burden imposed on government. It is, rather, the message and mission of government. The idea to build a new Indiana State Museum was a political idea in this sense, in the finest, most long-term and public-spirited meaning of the word. But it took a lot of politicking to get it done.

The first, last and greatest political hurdle was convincing the General Assembly that the state needed a Museum worthy of the name, and needed it enough to write a multi-million-dollar check. Even if the legislature might be persuaded, political reality required that primary support must come from the governor's office. Why? The Museum would almost certainly be built in the capital city, in Indianapolis. If introduced in the General Assembly by a central Indiana legislator, the Museum project would be fatally perceived as serving mostly local interests. Yet the chances of an Elkhart or Evansville legislator proposing the project were little or none. This left the governor's office as the only political power capable of advancing the idea. Fortunately, Indiana has had some far-sighted governors in recent decades.

After the 1957 Commission report failed to excite action in the General Assembly, Gov. Harold Handley (1957-61) sought out allies to advance the idea. He found them in what might have seemed an unlikely organization: the Junior League of Indianapolis. In 1959 the good women of the League formed the "History on the Move" project. Its mission and public benefit: Comb through the collections, identify significant

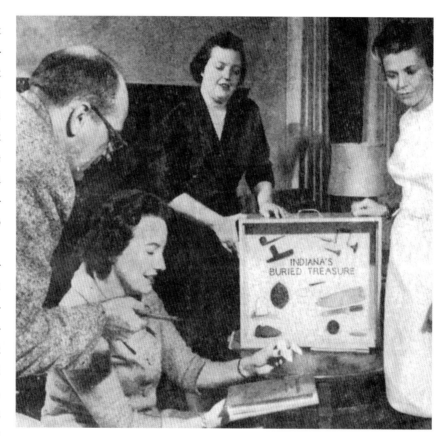

In a 1960 meeting, R. D. Starrett, the Museum's first full-time director, works with members of the Indianapolis Junior League's History on the Move Committee, (l-r) Mrs. Helen Noland, Mrs. Linda McLaughlin and Mrs.

Shirli Throop. Committee members were key contributors of time, energy and vision during the late 1950s and into the '60s and '70s as the Museum slowly evolved into a modern institution.

Right: At the behest of the Indianapolis Junior League's History on the Move Committee, Indianapolis architect Robert C. Hollingsworth drew this speculative image in 1962 to generate enthusiasm for a new museum building.

Below: Governor Matthew E. Welsh (1961-65)

Bottom: Governor Roger D. Branigin (1965-69)

artifacts, document them, then design and build traveling display cases for educational visits to public schools throughout the city and state. In relatively short order, the History on the Move Committee realized this was beyond their capacity either as curators or carpenters. Committee member Jan Finney remembered they found the basement museum in "miserable condition. It was mostly a lot of dusty stuffed birds. There were still some interesting things in boxes, but every time we discovered something really good, it would disappear. I think most of it wound up in some legislator's office."

So, somewhat ironically, the Committee refocused its efforts on the General Assembly. As stated in the 1959 annual report of the League's Project Planning Committee, "We hope that through this program, some pride and interest will be stimulated in the history of Indiana, and also in making provision for a much needed modern State Historical Museum."

Committee members attended meetings of other historical interest groups, talked one-on-one with state and city leaders, and even asked the Lilly Endowment to fund the hiring of a professionally-trained museum director. To catalyze discussion, the Committee asked League husband and local architect Robert C. Hollingsworth to design and fabricate a model of what a new museum might look like. Three years of promoting the idea culminated in a Committee tour of state museums in Frankfort, Kentucky and Springfield, Illinois, as well as museums in Bloomington and Ft. Wayne, IN. They went "in order to become acquainted with modern museum practices and to discuss the problems with well qualified men in this field," as the 1962 annual report explained. (A generation later, the planners of the new Indiana State Museum would take a similar tour, executed on a grander scale geographically but identical in spirit.)

Sometimes timing is everything. In 1962, just as the League's official efforts were drawing to a close, the City of

After World War II, under the leadership of Gov. Ralph F. Gates (1945-49) serious discussions of a new museum facility began floating around the highest levels of political power.

Indianapolis announced its intentions of building a shining, blandly modern City-County Building on Market Street. The old City Hall at 202 North Alabama Street was put up for sale. Real estate developers reacted with near-unanimous indifference to the prospect of remodeling the structure for the purposes of modern business.

The late Herbert Hill, one-time editor of *The Indianapolis News* and longstanding Republican Party powerbroker, once claimed that he was the first to suggest what became in hindsight the obvious solution: Move the Indiana State Museum into City Hall. Led by Helen Noland, who knew her way around the Democratic political infrastructure behind governors Matthew E. Welsh (1961-65) and Roger D. Branigin (1965-69), the History on the Move veterans lobbied quietly but constantly for the move. Finally in the mid-late '60s, the state officially extended an offer and the city accepted. The Museum doors opened to the public in 1967. Gov. Branigin paid for a brochure called "Doors to Tomorrow" to promote museum tours and solicit private donations. League stalwarts joined with other supporters to form the Indiana State Museum Society. The modern era had dawned.

The Museum flourished in the bright light, attracting an enthusiastic new audience and, not surprisingly, a huge increase in significant donations of artifacts. Even in its capacious new facilities, the Museum was becoming a victim of its own success and running out of room and resources. Further, new conservation technologies, new techniques in exhibition design and new emphasis on educational services – all ideas the basement Museum might never have considered – were now within plausible reach. The larger space had enlarged the Museum's vision of itself and the public's vision, as well. The Indianapolis firm of Wright, Porteous and Lowe com-pleted conceptual designs for a second museum structure, a modernist tower to be built on the empty lot immediately north of the Museum. Not surprisingly, the legislature was unenthusiastic about another major upgrade so soon after the last.

But the legislature did get at least a little excited by another project, the White River State Park. Although the idea of a recreational space on the banks of White River west of downtown goes back at least to Indianapolis' Central Business District development plan of 1958, the White River State Park was born conceptually in the mid-1970s. Then, the so-called "City Committee," a bipartisan group of political and business leaders, generated a broad consensus about the need to develop a state park in this space, with an NFL-class stadium as the primary tenant. They built a case strong enough to persuade the Lilly Endowment to contribute $5 million to acquire the 250 acres that today comprise the park. In 1979, Indianapolis lawyer Theodore Boehm wrote the legislation by which the General Assembly established the White River State Park.

In 1981, Robert D. Orr became governor after serving two terms as Otis Bowen's lieutenant governor. Orr, a successful businessman and legislator, and a fourth-generation Hoosier from the Evansville area, had grown up in a family that emphasized the value of education and global experience. During his two terms as governor, Orr campaigned hard for initiatives that would promote Indiana on the international stage. On the home front that meant supporting a series of high-energy – if perhaps low plausibility – schemes from both public and private sectors to develop the White River Park. Central to any development was, in Orr's mind, a new Indiana State Museum.

Below: The imposing Indianapolis City Hall, designed in 1910 by Rubush and Hunter, became the Indiana State Museum in 1967. Bottom Left: The floor pattern beneath the original pendulum location.

"We needed a showcase for Indiana," Orr remembered, "a place to take a visiting political leader or industrialist and show them what Indiana was all about. This was a new day. Indiana had to take its place at the center of the stage or we'd get lost in the crowd of competing states."

"But it was clear that the old Indianapolis City Hall was just not the right place for the Museum. To function effectively, a museum building has to be built as a museum. The legislature understood all of this, but at that time, during that economy, a new Indiana State Museum in the new White River State Park was not going to be a popular project. There would always be some degree of anti-Indianapolis sentiment holding it back. For some legislators a new museum in a new park in Indianapolis would never be as important as a highway bridge in their district. In the end, though, they understood and we moved ahead."

A proposed expansion to the Museum's facility at 202 North Alabama Street, prepared by the Indianapolis architectural firm of Wright, Porteous and Lowe in 1976.

SCHOOL NO. 5 FAÇADE

Although the Indiana State Museum is a thoroughly modern design inside and out, one significant interior wall – in fact the first wall to greet visitors as they pass through the main entrance – was built in 1922.

Rising three stories above the lobby, this historic front façade of Indianapolis Public School's Oscar C. McCulloch School No. 5 stands as an impressive reminder of the city's and state's social and ethnic heritage. The school was named for the Reverend Oscar C. McCullogh (1843-1891), pastor of the Plymouth Congregational Church and an early advocate of social services and populist causes. Under his leadership, Plymouth became the most progressive church in the city and established programs including the Summer Mission for Sick Children (sometimes called the Fresh Air Mission), a free kindergarten, the city's first training school for nurses, and an orphanage for boys.

Over the decades, School No. 5 served the city's most diverse neighborhood, bringing together a population of Slovakian, Romanian, Greek, Lithuanian, Bulgarian, Hungarian, Appalachian whites, Gypsies, Chinese and African-American students. To symbolize this global perspective and to impart a beautiful vision of American citizenship, the school was graced with an exceptional set of decorative details, most notably the twin terracotta hemispheres flanking the main entrance, now reinstalled directly to the right of the Museum's main entrance.

It is this decoration more than any other factor that distinguished the design by Indianapolis architect Robert Frost Daggett and, indirectly, doomed the building to destruction – and eventual resurrection.

In 1984, as enthusiasm for the development of White River State Park was building, early park planners realized that School No. 5, empty but still standing a few yards north of Washington Street in the middle of park property, presented a considerable obstacle to development. In particular, its presence made it nearly impossible to develop the underground parking structure intended for the site. The historic preservation community had already announced their intention of challenging in court any plan to demolish the school and its significant decorations.

Park planners decided the best solution was an out-of-court "settlement." They hired a demolition crew to plow into the structure in the dead of night, inflicting sufficient damage to preclude any hope of salvaging it – or so they hoped.

The preservationists fought back. Joined by other community leaders now galvanized by the preemptory tactics of the park development commission, Historic Landmarks Foundation of Indiana successfully sued to prevent further destruction of the remaining school walls and to reclaim any extant pieces that may have already been removed. After a protracted process, the court approved a plan that obliged the park commission to gently deconstruct what was left of the school, store it and, in a fitting act of architectural justice, reconstruct it as part of the new state museum intended for the site in some unspecified future.

Most preservationists assumed that this future design would incorporate the School No. 5 façade as an exterior element. Bill Browne of Ratio Architects, a relatively young, preservation-minded architectural firm working hard to establish its reputation, took it upon himself to propose another solution to Reid Williamson, head of the Landmarks Foundation. Unsolicited and unpaid, Browne designed and built a small model demonstrating how the School No. 5 façade might be included as an interior wall. A decade later, the unspecified future became quite specific; and far from being an up-and-coming firm, Ratio had arrived as architects of the Indiana State Museum. Browne dusted off his model and began rebuilding history.

Opposite Page, Left to Right: The evolution of School No. 5: from the freestanding edifice that served thousands of children as Oscar C. McCulloch School, Indianapolis Public School No. 5; through its 1984 demolition; as first conceived by Ratio Architects in its 1985 speculations for the future Indiana State Museum; and (below) finally as it stands today in the Museum's Grand Lobby, once again serving Indiana's children.

INDIANA STATE MUSEUM

"To function effectively, a museum building has
to be built as a museum."

Robert D. Orr, Governor, 1981-89

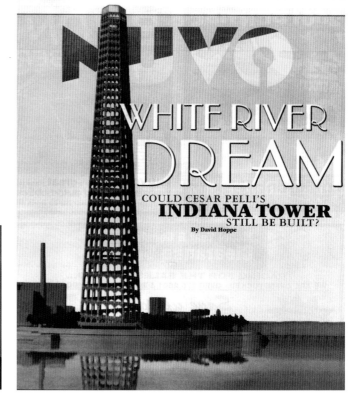

*Left: Governor Robert D. Orr
(1981-89) Center: Governor Evan
Bayh (1989-97) Right: As part of
the White River State Park vision
plan developed in the early 1980s,
internationally renown architect
Cesar Pelli designed this 750-ft.-
high tower, shown here in a 2001
publication of NUVO, speculating
on its possible realization 20 years
later. The tower's purpose: Enjoy
the view and punctuate the
landscape.*

A significant step toward a mature vision of the Park came with the convening in 1981 of a group of internationally respected designers and planners to help the state conceptualize this resource. This group included Charles Moore, Cesar Pelli and Angela Danadjieva, names to conjure in professional discussions if perhaps unfamiliar to most Hoosiers. They painted a grand picture, including a fabulous observation tower rising hundreds of feet above the landscape, and generated considerable public excitement, which was really the point. In the early 1980s, the Museum and the Park needed that energy, to move into the future.

Helping to lead the charge – indeed, the man probably shouting loudest – was the new director of the Museum, Lee Scott Theisen. Orr had hired Theisen, the first non-Hoosier and the first museum professional to lead the institution, to signal the start of a new era. "It was obvious that the Gov. wanted to move the Museum forward and that he expected me to take the initiative," Theisen said. "The institution had been fairly mori-

bund for several years and it was clear to me that my job was to create a much higher public profile and jack up the buzz."

Indeed. One of Theisen's first moves after assuming office was to repaint the office a canary yellow bright enough to require sunglasses. Theisen thought it was entirely within the Museum staff's capabilities to open two major exhibitions on the same day, then do it again two months later. And those shows covered a panorama of subjects geared to attract new audiences to the Museum, subjects ranging from art to African-American history, from Barbie dolls to Amish quilts to lingerie. If Gov. Orr understood that Indiana was now competing with its neighboring states on an international stage, Theisen knew that the Museum was now competing with "blockbuster shows in other cities and, for that matter, with Disney World, for people's time, attention and dollars." He was fond of quoting Columbian Exposition master planner Daniel Burnham: "Make no small plans, they have no magic to stir men's blood" – or jack up the buzz.

With Orr's urging and Theisen's high-energy attitude leading the way, the Indiana State Museum board voted in 1984 to relocate the Museum to the developing White River State Park.

Left: The conceptual design for the Museum by E. Verner Johnson and the Indianapolis firm CSO.

With Orr's urging and Theisen's high-energy attitude leading the way, the Indiana State Museum board voted in 1984 to relocate the Museum to the developing White River State Park. To lend some substance to the dream, Theisen hired respected architect E. Verner Johnson, a Boston-based museum specialist, to develop the new Museum's program, the functional space and flow chart for the future facility. This would prove to be a protracted labor, lasting more than a decade and would eventually be completed without either Theisen or Johnson. Whatever the shortcomings or extravagances that would lead to his invited resignation, Theisen imparted a bit of his Burnham-esque, perhaps Barnum-esque, spirit to the institution, and showed the state and the staff a new way to look at their Museum. But in the late 1980s, it was still a distant view.

The entire Park project, including the Museum, suffered a terrible setback on September 11, 1992 when four key Park supporters – Mike Carroll of the Lilly Endowment; Frank McKinney of Bank One; Robert Welch, executive director of the White River State Park Development Commission; and longtime political rainmaker John Weliever – were killed in a plane crash while on Park business. This tragedy profoundly shook the Indianapolis community. For the next two years, Park and Museum progress seemed stuck in neutral, prompting one insider to complain that "no one appeared to be driving the bus." Yet progress was made, most of it slow and behind the scenes, some of it quite public, including the altogether successful opening of Victory Field on Park property.

In 1995 came the announcement that the state, with support from the Lilly Endowment, would build an IMAX Theater on the Museum site just west of the Eiteljorg Museum. It was commonly understood that ultra-large-screen theaters never succeed as stand-alone facilities, and that sooner or later the Indiana State Museum would necessarily be attached. But politically speaking the $9.5 million theater was an easier, which is to say cheaper, sell than

Behind the random ashlar limestone and stainless steel of the Museum's south façade once stood the masses of the first IMAX theater design (top). Although planned as part of a unified museum structure, the theater was built as a standalone structure, anticipating an eastern half designed in much the same stolid style. Ratio Architects realized the theater would need to be reclad and the lobby removed to best incorporate it within the revitalized aesthetic and programmatic vision of the Museum.

the complete theater-Museum package, which would require an estimated $65 million for Museum construction, plus an additional $40 million to be raised privately for the exhibitions. This might be considered the tail wagging the dog, but Indiana architects heard the barking and knew that any proposal to design the theater was really a proposal to design the Museum. The race to win the architectural commission began in earnest.

Architecture is hardly a stranger to politics. On a hammer-and-nails level, buildings always require some degree of governmental approval to make sure they are "built to code." Often buildings in recognized historic districts require other layers of bureaucratic and aesthetic review. Even after legislatures and governors have given the go-ahead, the designs of important public buildings are reviewed in the court of public opinion. And this makes most politicians cautious. Unlike other governmental programs launched with fanfare then forgotten in implementation, significant buildings stand as lasting and obvious reminders of the brilliance or mediocrity of their design – and those who commissioned it.

If pressed, most politicians would echo the late Larry Conrad, one-time Indiana Secretary of State and a trustee of the Museum, who frequently spoke in expansive terms of the need for major state buildings to offer inspiration. Perhaps more than any elected official in recent memory, the late Gov. Frank O'Bannon went beyond the echo. He realized that a building's ability to inspire was not simply an intangible quality to be added, if possible, to its functionality. It was, in fact, its function. As State Office Building Commission Director Susan Williams remembered, "He repeatedly told me that the people of Indiana needed and deserved a State Museum that would inspire them to face this new century with confidence. I believe in his mind this was the new building's fundamental purpose."

One does not contract for inspiration on a low-bid basis. In the past, in their attempts to win such major commissions, Indiana architects have generally allied themselves with nationally or internationally known architects with more "inspiring" credentials. This makes good Hoosier sense on a functional level. When designing a library, hotel or museum, choose an architect with library, hotel or museum experience. If museum architects are rare in Indiana, find one somewhere else. From one perspective, the search for nationally or internationally acclaimed architects made perfect sense for a city and state hungry for broader perception as a "world-class" place. From another, this sent a not-so-subtle message to local architects: If you were good enough to win the commission for the Indiana State Museum, you would have already won a major museum commission somewhere else. For better or worse, and however self-deprecating, most Hoosier architects assumed they would need a "bigname" out-of-state designer to lead the team.

The other political truth that Indiana architects understood as unavoidable: that outside ally or allies would need experience in IMAX and museum design. With a resume that included the planning of over 140 history museums, art centers, science centers and IMAX theaters, as well as the 10-year-old program space plan for the Indiana State Museum, E. Verner Johnson seemed to be the only name, big or otherwise, on the list. Johnson was actually asked to head up several competing teams organized by Indiana firms. He accepted all invitations and waited to see who would win, secure in the knowledge that he would.

The team that won the contract was headed by CSO, a 40-year-old Indianapolis firm, with Johnson subcontracted as the design architect, principal crafter of the building's look and feel. Work began with the goal to open the theater before the end of the Bayh administration in 1996. As expected, the Museum and the IMAX would be designed as a single building with the theater constructed first.

When conceptual drawings of the entire project were released, public reaction was, in a word, restrained. This was certainly not to fault Johnson's overall competence and understanding of the technical rigors of modern museum design. Rather, any criticism came as faint praise, which ran the short gamut from "nice" to "OK." The conceptual images were seen as aesthetically solid, a perfectly acceptable design by a thoroughly competent architect. But the design seemed to lack any intrinsic quality that bespoke Indiana, however elusive such ideas might be. It felt somewhat interchangeable with other designs by Johnson, perhaps an unavoidable problem when using an architect with that much museum experience. Apart from such intangible matters, the Johnson-CSO team deserves credit for identifying and in some cases resolving some of the very tangible difficulties arising from

The decision to change architects in mid-project sent a powerful message to the architectural community. As Williams had stressed to O'Bannon and in several public statements, the Indiana State Museum deserved an Indiana architect to lead the design.

the challenge of placing this monumental structure on its restrictive site. Among others, the idea to locate the Museum's administrative wing west of the canal comes from these original planning efforts.

In November of 1996, Lt. Gov. Frank O'Bannon was elected governor in his own right, and a month later the IMAX Theater opened in White River State Park. O'Bannon announced that his administration was committed to building a grand new Indiana State Museum adjacent to the theater, that it would be a source of pride for all Hoosiers, and that it would serve as a touchstone for an energetic education policy. The mood at the beginning of his administration was high. All factors seemed aligned. The state was solid financially – thanks in large part to the billion-dollar surplus left by the Bayh administration – a design team had been named. In June, 1997, the General Assembly approved the $65 million Museum construction budget, prompted by Gov. O'Bannon's firm communication that the state's total budget would go unsigned without the Museum appropriation. Yet for some reason, progress on the new Museum design was slow, at times imperceptible.

On August 1, 1997, management of the Museum project was taken over by the newly appointed director of the State Office Building Commission, Susan Williams. A long-time member of the Indianapolis City-County Council, Williams had seen her downtown district through years of urban rebirth. Although she had never managed a design and construction development of this or-any scale, Williams was a take-charge style of leader well schooled in the motivation of personnel and the navigation of bureaucracies. Gov. O'Bannon had asked her to get this project off the dime, and she intended to do just that.

However certain Williams was of her role, the change of project leadership may have left the architectural team uncertain of its role and perhaps wary of someone who might turn out to be just the latest manager. Any project of this magnitude and symbolic importance demands an unusually high degree of harmony among all participants. The miscommunications and miscalculations impossible to avoid in large projects can only be smoothed by an evolving sense of shared vision and common purpose.

By April, 1998, it became clear that Williams and the design team were miles apart on critical issues and not moving closer. Williams grew increasingly concerned that the project would not come together on schedule, on budget or, aesthetically speaking, on target. She met with Gov. O'Bannon and explained the situation. On April 21, Williams met with the designers and terminated the relationship.

This was an unprecedented and gutsy decision, potentially career-ending if the project were to slow even further, which was quite possible now that a new architect would have to be hired and a new design generated. It would have been politically easier to placate, conciliate and smooth things over, but O'Bannon didn't. He made the hard call by trusting Williams to make the hard call.

The decision to change architects in mid-project sent a powerful message to the architectural community. As Williams had stressed to O'Bannon and in several public statements, the Indiana State Museum deserved an Indiana architect to lead the design. Not just a Hoosier firm to prepare the construction drawings and wade through the day-to-day details of building the building – that had already been stipulated in the enabling legislation – but a Hoosier firm to envision and design the look and feel of the institution. This was a

Upper Left, Clockwise:
Historic Landmarks Foundation
of Indiana headquarters,
Indianapolis.
Cummins Engine Company Parts
Distribution Center, Indianapolis.
Emmis Communications World
Headquarters, Indianapolis.
Indiana University Radio
and Television Building,
Bloomington, IN.
Over the course of its 22-year
history, Ratio Architects, Inc.
has brought to bear an array
of stylistic skills and sensibilities
to fulfill a wide range of client
missions: from traditional to
contemporary; from the historical
to the technological. In the process,
the firm has evolved a unifying
respect for design and appropriate
use of materials to best embody the
client institution.

decision of crucial symbolic importance, founded on the twin beliefs that the state had the right stuff architecturally to design a structure of this magnitude and importance, and that only an Indiana architect would truly feel the Museum's meaning and spirit. This was something new for Indiana architects: a vote of unparalleled confidence, a $65 million vote of confidence.

It probably required a political veteran to make such an impolitic decision. Had Williams been a career bureaucrat or museum professional, she most probably would not have chosen to rock the political boat so dangerously. As it was, powerful people, particularly O'Bannon, knew her and trusted her judgment and trusted that she would somehow make it all happen. On April 22, the day after the governor approved her decision, Williams made three calls to three Indiana architectural firms. The interview process was short, the decision swift. By the end of the week, Williams picked Bill Browne and Ratio Architects to take over the design process. Thrilled but daunted, Browne gathered his senior colleagues and discussed their best course of action. As Browne said, "This was a five-year project at best, and we had four years to do it. Susan had promised the Governor opening day would be in May, 2002, and she was going to deliver. And that meant we were going to deliver."

Left: Seen from the Northwest, the Museum graces the historic Indianapolis Water Company Canal.

THE L.S. AYRES TEA ROOM

For nearly 90 years, the Tea Room atop the L.S. Ayres Department Store in downtown Indianapolis symbolized a way of life that was at once urban and urbane, elegant yet democratic in its appeal and access. These images still resonate with Hoosiers: Luncheon on white linen for ladies in gloves and hats; crystal and silver and please and thank you; a trip to the capital city for a panoramic day of shopping; the richest chicken soup ever ladled into a china bowl; a dessert born of fairy tales and a treasure chest for children.

Although the Tea Room closed in 1990, and the building redesigned as part of the Circle Centre Mall, its elegant spirit remained. As plans for the new Indiana State Museum began to take shape in the mid-1990s, members of the Ayres family joined with the family of former Ayres CEO, Daniel F. Evans, Sr. to encourage a recreated Tea Room in the Museum. Thanks to this support, the Tea Room evolved dramatically from its initial concept as a modest extension of the Crossroads Café on the northwest corner of the Museum's second floor. The architects reconfigured the entire design of the Museum's western second floor, doubling the Tea Room's square-footage and repositioning it as a standalone space with authentic period furnishings and recreations. A nearly full complement of original Tea Room tables and chairs was located in a restaurant in Culver, IN, and the architects persuaded the owner to trade these for new furniture, plus the tax advantages of the donated originals. Drapery and carpet were recreated from samples cannily saved by the Museum when the Ayres store closed.

With a reborn menu including the Tea Room's legendary "chicken velvet soup" and the "snow princess" meringue and ice-cream dessert, as well as a photomural of downtown Indianapolis peeking through the Tea Room's windows, the trip into history became a true re-enactment.

So true to the spirit and feel of the original, in fact, that today the L.S. Ayres Tea Room continues to attract thousands of visitors, and is nearly sold out during the year-end holiday season months in advance.

Then and now: The Tea Room in Indianapolis' L.S. Ayres & Co. department store was a favorite luncheon spot for generations of Hoosiers. A decade after its official closing, the recreated Tea Room on the Museum's second floor continues to attract thousands of visitors throughout the year.

DESIGNING THE MUSEUM

For Bill Browne and Ratio, this was the chance of a career – chancy, indeed. A five-year project due in four years. The largest project Ratio had ever attempted. The firm's first museum, for that matter, its first cultural institution. And a Governor who had vowed there would be an Indiana State Museum standing in the White River State Park in the spring of 2002, "come hell or high water," as he said to a group of Museum contributors. Pressure?

Almost from the moment he got off the phone with Williams, Browne knew that the new Museum would be modernist. Looking back, Browne remembered this decision felt so intuitively obvious he never seriously questioned it. But people familiar with Ratio's resume might have, or at least arched an eyebrow. From the time Browne established the firm in the early 1980s, Ratio had built an impeccable reputation for its rehabilitations and sympathetic additions to a long string of historic structures. When Historic Landmarks Foundation of Indiana, one of the premier preservationist organizations in the country, hired Ratio to

design its Indianapolis headquarters in 1990, the firm's historicist credentials were validated beyond question. And that made Browne's decision to design a modernist museum that much easier. Only a bona fide historicist might propose a modernist design and speak confidently of its meaning, of the need for a design pointed to the future rather than the past.

But first, back to school. With Hoosier historians leading the sessions, the Ratio team took a crash course in Indiana, everything from art to zoology, from folklore to statistics, and anything else the conversation suggested. They listened and looked, scribbled and sketched. Increasingly convinced the Museum could tell the story of Hoosier industry, particularly

Above Left: The limestone that clads the Empire State Building was carved from the heart of Indiana's bedrock, seen here at the Empire Quarry. This coming together of megalithic wall, reflective water and verdant foliage formed the foundational vision for Ratio's design concept of the Museum's identity.

Above Right: The beehive kilns of Cayuga, IN inspired the metal banding of the Museum's soaring brick cylinder. Bricks used in the reconstructed façade of School No. 5 were manufactured at this facility.

Opposite Page: From the quarry exhibit at the eastern tip of the Museum, visitors see the Statehouse and the larger context of the capital city's skyline. The General Assembly considered this view to be sacrosanct when funding Museum construction and mandated a perpetual "view corridor" or visual easement to protect it.

MODERNISM

Architecturally, the Indiana State Museum should be considered a modernist building. Although the word is often used to describe a broad type of buildings – generally those that emphasize geometric masses, relatively unadorned planar surfaces and, particularly in large structures, expansive use of regular grids – modernism means more. Modernism comprises a collection of styles inspired by a search for honesty in structural expression, catalyzed by the familiar idea that form follows function. This is complemented by the almost metaphysical quest for pure, or universal forms. At the socio-political level, modernism stems from the desire to find a basic architectural vocabulary of forms that might be applied equally to buildings large and small, grand and humble, public and private. Each of these perspectives has contributed to the evolution of modernism.

As an identifiable movement with supporters and critics, modernism is almost a century old – begging the question of when its name becomes a misnomer. In that time modernism has been trumpeted as the hope of the future and the common people's only chance of achieving urban dignity. It has also been denounced as a soul-less style better suited to factories than human institutions. It has been promoted as the only appropriate style for an energetic, post-WWII America; then quickly dismissed as a tired aesthetic mired in orthodoxy and rote practice.

In its most energetic historical moments, modernism has been fueled by a nearly utopian optimism, and promoted as the architectural vehicle of true social equality. Similarly, its expansive use of glass bespeaks the spirit of institutional openness and clarity. Even those who bemoan its denuding of historical ornament respect its visual purity, at times seeing it as a distilled subspecies of classicism. Those who neither rally to its social meaning nor thrill to its geometric harmonies at least applaud the efficiency of its construction. Because of its reliance on the fundamental unit of construction – upright posts spanned by horizontal beams – modernism has proven adaptable to almost every regional material or style of architecture, from limestone in Indiana to adobe in Arizona. As monolithic as it may appear to its critics, modernism actually encompasses a wide range of variations both bold and subtle.

Although modernist theory was initially propounded in Europe during the first decades of the 20th century, many would argue its inspiration was the unadorned geometries of earlier American industry, of the factories, foundries, mills and silos built too large, too economically and too quickly for ornamentation – a bit like this country itself. Later, as American cities sprawled across their gridded landscape, the gridded forms of modernism became the obvious building blocks and landmarks. By the late 1950s, modernism had won. While much of the world was still rebuilding from the war, or struggling to bring modern technology to pre-industrial cultures, modernism was the accepted, indeed appropriate style for a new and improved America in a new and improving world. It was the style of all things modern in the most modern nation on earth.

More than merely up-to-date, it was the look of the future, of a better world. It became the architectural style of science fiction, as well as shopping malls. It was used to design space-age churches pointing us to the heavens, as well as the fleet of new public schools designed to handle the deluge of Baby Boom children. It was then, and remains today, the architecture of confidence in the future, the style of hope.

Above: Ratio designed this window onto the Museum's third-floor art galleries as a tribute to modernist master Marcel Breuer's Whitney Museum of American Art in New York. From the galleries, the window frames a landscape view of Military Park, echoing the Hoosier School paintings hanging a few feet away.

Left: Whether expressed as spidery, almost conceptual frameworks of space or the defining bones and muscles of massed construction, the modernist aesthetic forms the unifying design harmonies of the Museum. The 19-bay stretch of the entrance canopy, emblematic of Indiana's position as the 19th state admitted to the union, contrasts but complements the brick tower as it meets the quarry exhibit curtain wall.

Right: After visiting the J. Paul Getty Museum in Los Angeles, the Museum design team came back inspired by the rich textural variety of light and shade made possible by roughback travertine marble.

Far Right: Ratio maximized this variety by using a random ashlar pattern of stone placement.

Opposite Page: The north façade of the Museum displays the full spectrum of the state's architectural materials: limestone, sandstone, steel, aluminum, glass and brick.

in its use of materials, the team began an episodic pilgrimage to sites around the state – to quarries, brickworks and steel mills. At the end of July, hoping to expand their education beyond the state of Indiana to the state of the modern museum, Browne, Williams, Indiana State Architect Sheila Snider, Museum Director Dick Gantz and other members of the Museum leadership team went on an intensive four-city museum inspection to Minneapolis, St. Paul, Sacramento and Los Angeles. (Later in the design process, various members of the team would also visit other museums in New York City, Raleigh, Grand Rapids, Tacoma, Seattle, Mashantucket, Connecticut and Washington, D.C., as well as Indianapolis.) According to Williams, each trip gave the team "renewed understanding" of the challenge faced. By October, the team was ready to present their stories,

images and thematic interpretations first to the Governor and, a few days later, to leaders of the Lilly Endowment. The Governor was delighted. The Endowment would become the Museum's most significant supporter in the private sector.

It may sound strange to speak of a building's story, of its themes and metaphors, but great buildings arise when architects understand their mission in the most powerful metaphoric terms, when they understand not just what a building can be but what it needs to be on a metaphoric level – of what it needs to mean more than look like. That is what Ratio was able to communicate so successfully to the Governor and the Endowment, and shortly thereafter, to the people of Indiana in a series of public presentations.

The theme and spirit of the Museum was ordered around three key concepts, three crucial stories of Hoosier history and

BRIDGE TO THE FUTURE

One of the challenges of the site was the constraint imposed on the footprint of the Museum site by the historic Water Company Canal. Moving the canal was never considered. That would be too expensive, and the Park had just spent $10 million to redesign it in this configuration. Further, the canal had far too much historic significance to tinker with: Any re-redesign would involve endless bureaucratic processing. Constructed in the 1830s the canal was the last section of an ambitious 19th century network to connect Lake Erie to the frontier. Although useful to locals, the Indiana section proved to be a financial disaster for the state and the canal was never fully developed. Abandoned as a means of transportation, the canal was all but forgotten until the 1990s, when the White River State Park Development Commission hired Sasaki Associates of Massachusetts and devoted $10 million to an elegant redesign of the canal as it passed through the park and down to the river. The canal project was a major asset, elevating the aesthetic tone of the entire park and attracting tens of thousands of visitors to the park as a park.

In order to achieve the square footage needed, the architects would have to either design a higher building or locate some museum functions in a separate pavilion. For any number of practical and psychological reasons, the prevailing wisdom of museum design strongly argued against vertical expansion. The first architectural team had considered the situation and opted for a western pavilion with a straightforward bridge as a workable connection. Ratio agreed that a separate structure to the west was best, but felt the bridge deserved a more meaningful design solution. After researching the historic bridges of Indiana, the Ratio team decided to recreate a Whipple Truss Bridge, a design used throughout Indiana in the 19th and early 20th centuries, characterized by diagonal rods that distribute the structural stresses for maximum strength and efficiency. And, of course, the bridge would want to be aligned with the 9.5 degree angle of the old National Road (see drawing on page 55), forming a nearly 400 foot corridor from the center of the Grand Lobby west to Tomorrow's Indiana, the gallery of the future.

The Whipple Truss Bridge (Right) connecting the main Museum to the Administration Building to the west pays homage to Indiana's historic steel bridges (above)and, metaphorically, the main expansion westward of the population in the 19th century. Just as these Americans saw their future to the west, the Museum addresses our state's future at the end of this bridge, in an exhibit titled "Tomorrow's Indiana." Below: A bridge "knuckle" viewed before installation. Below Right: Hanging the bridge.

culture. First was the idea of Hoosier spirit and character. The Museum design should give form to that endless dialogue of opposing sensibilities, the closed and exuberant, the rustic and urbane, the cautious and the entrepreneurial. That basic tension fueled the entire design.

The second large theme arose from Indiana's history of certain elemental building materials – stone and steel, glass and brick. It was widely understood that the design would include significant amounts of limestone. How much and where was yet to be determined. Once the decision was made to create the massive south façade, it became clear that other smaller visual blocks of smooth or dressed limestone would balance this – and thus were conceived the northern-facing pavilions, as well as the limestone on the detached administration wing. And once that decision was made, the architects realized that it made more thematic sense, and offered more design opportunity, to conceive the Museum as a series of connected but independent containers each characterized by a dominant use of one of the state's indigenous materials. This harmonized with the team's understanding that Indiana history was, in so many ways, the story of these materials, of their economics and the culture of the regions that produced them, from rural limestone to the urban steel. As their designs evolved, the architects decided to let the state's materials "speak for themselves," as it were, in stand alone elements of a collaged rather than homogenized design. Continuity between elements would be created by the repeated use of surface pattern or structural geometry.

As such, when the architects found the chance to use Indiana sandstone, they realized it would provide the perfect counterpoint to the limestone if arranged in a similar "random ashlar" pattern of rectangular blocks of different sizes fitted together seemingly at random. The sandstone used in the Museum comes from Mansfield, in Parke County, where

the Chicago Brownstone Company once thrived, shipping its stone around the country for "brownstone" apartment buildings during the late 19th century. Just as Ratio was formulating its design concepts in 1998, the Mansfield Stone Company was being created to reinvigorate this historic Indiana resource. Its palette of warm brown, wheat, beige and burgundy allowed Ratio to design the Museum's northwest pavilion as a lovely complement to the limestone, glass and brick of the rest of the building.

Through stone to steel to glass, the geometric rhythms of the south façade bring syncopated unity to the Museum's palette of materials.

The use of glass was inevitable. In the Museum it is used somewhat symbolically to represent the great period of Indiana's glass industry, which came and went over a few decades at the end of the 19th and beginning of the 20th centuries. But today glass is so much a part of the world that it has become nearly invisible, conceptually as well as physically. Glass, as much if not more than steel, creates the possibility of architectural modernism. It gives architects the ability to construct walls that provide containment and shelter but are visually all but absent. Glass walls are not structure; they are windows made grandiose and invitations to think beyond the box of the building. In the Museum, this is an invitation to see the state – and, at the eastern end of the building, to see the Statehouse.

The marriage of site and structure is unavoidable, but their relationship is a matter of design.

The eastern element of the Museum assemblage grows out of two strong design ideas, so strong as to be practically mandates. First, the State Capitol steps must be prominently visible from the third floor of the Museum. Second, as the public had repeatedly suggested through a series of community discussions around the state in the earliest stages of the museum fund-raising, they wanted the Museum to contain a recreation of a limestone quarry. The solution was a trapezoidal wall of glass, a smaller version of the Grand Lobby's north façade. From the Statehouse, the view west between twin office buildings centers on that dark trapezoid. It is one of Browne's favorite aspects of the Museum design. Commanding yet restless, the dark shape rivets the viewer's attention while its odd angles keep it from feeling symmetrical and settled.

An historic drawing of the National Road bridge across the White River.

The use of glass in the Museum was also the source of great tension in establishing the institution's architectural identity. The significant expanses of glass cladding various elements of the Museum testify to its mission as a public gathering place, a space enclosed but still engaged in visual dialogue with the rest of the city – and by extension, with the state and the world. Bountiful natural light, however appropriate to one aspect of the Museum's mission and certainly its history, blanches its conservational mission, best fulfilled by a hermetically-sealed depository of artifacts. Splitting the difference, the Ratio team opted for moveable louvers, glass tinting and filtering screens – notice the subtle dotting on the glass walls of the Whipple bridge – to reduce light levels while maintaining the Museum's visual openness.

The other "mandate" left to address: the Foucault pendulum. Originally purchased in the late 1960s for the Museum on North Alabama Street and ideally suited to that building's rotunda, the pendulum became a signature element of the institution. Its inclusion in the new building was another given for the Ratio team. The solution Ratio devised was to translate that cylindrical space into a brick-clad form with both interior and exterior faces. It is the highest structure in the Museum design and a chance for the architects to introduce

a strong vertical accent to an otherwise horizontal structure. Symbolically it is one of the most complex elements in the Museum. It embodies at once the state's grain silos and industrial smokestacks, as well as the once-thriving brick kilns of Indiana. (The Ratio team had visited the nation's last coal fired beehive kilns of the Colonial Brick Company in tiny Cayuga, Indiana and learned of its 100-year history and current national reputation as a maker of historical bricks for preservation projects.)

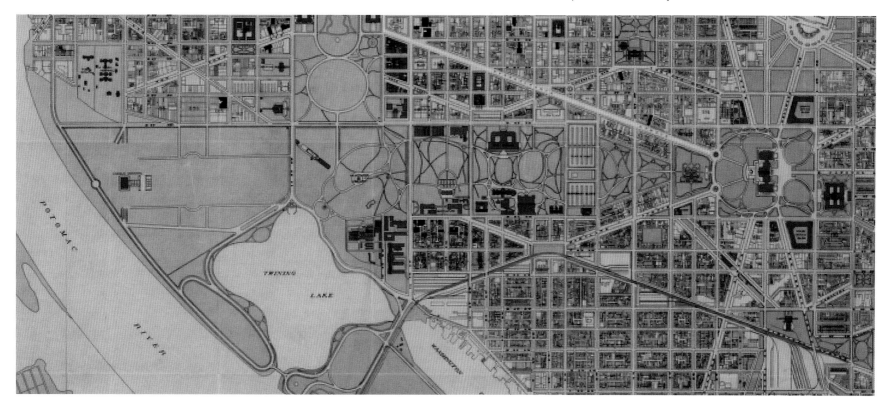

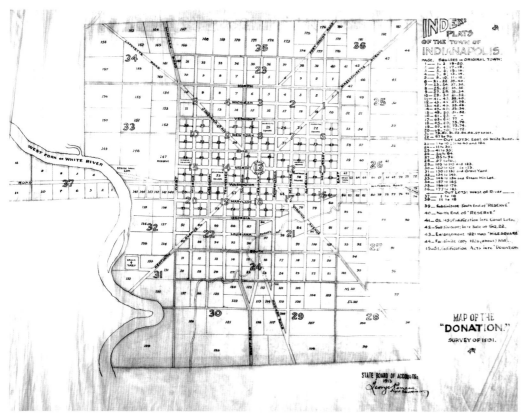

Above: Pierre Charles L'Enfant's 1791 plan of Washington, D.C. inspired his apprentice Alexander Ralston in his 1821 design of Indianapolis.

Left: In 1830 the National Road crossed the city east-to-west, angling 9.5 degrees to the north as it bent toward the shortest span across the White River. That bend began on the future site of the Indiana State Museum. Ratio's architects

embraced this angle first for its historic importance and ultimately for its symbolic expression of the skewed perspective intrinsic to Hoosier character.

Below: The Museum's plan geometry is derived primarily from the merger of the orthogonal Indianapolis city grid and the unique 9.5 degree angle of the Old National Road as it crossed what is now the Museum's front lawn.

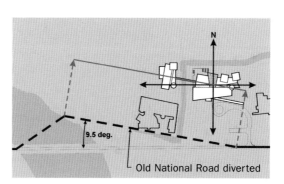

Right: The Museum presents a collage of diverse geometric masses as a unified whole.

Bottom Row: In the early stages of design conceptualization, the Ratio architects evolved their ideas of the Museum's main massing through several models. These experimental versions served a crucial role in the design's evolution, each suggesting possibilities that subsequent models refined or refuted or even recycled ideas previously rejected. Eventually the design came together through a combination of rational and intuitive resolution.

Bottom Right: The final model of the Museum synthesized the best of the earlier design explorations. It came into focus when the team moved the central Museum block to the south half of the site to let the sun play across the stoic limestone façade of the main entrance.

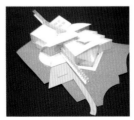 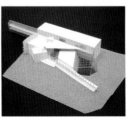 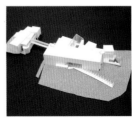 

When approaching the White River, surveyors determined the road required such a deviation. It was decided to bend the road 9.5 degrees to the north to best approach the river. That bend began precisely on the Museum site.

The third basic theme was the site itself – the place where the Museum would stand. For a building that was all about a place, all about the stories that comprise Indiana, Ratio realized that the idea of site was both literally and metaphorically the foundation of its design. In this, however modern or modernist the Museum might be, it cannot escape the essence of its art.

Vincent J. Scully, Jr., America's foremost teacher and historian of architecture for the last half century, explained the symbiosis of site and structure in his 1991 book, *Architecture: The Natural and the Manmade.* "The shape of architecture is the shape of the earth as it is modified by the structures of mankind….The first fact of architecture is the topography and the way human beings respond to it with their own constructed forms." The ultimate decision for architects is whether "to echo the shapes of the landscape or to contrast with them."

The marriage of site and structure is unavoidable, but their relationship is a matter of design. It can be a graceful pas-de-deux or a thoughtful debate – and Scully suggests that either approach can work. The Indiana State Museum succeeds in doing both, and thus achieves what is commonly called a strong "sense of place." This is a nebulous, perhaps overused phrase, but illuminating when accurate. True sense of place is the offspring of the rare marriage of site and structure that gives new meaning to both and translates one's limitations into the other's inspirations.

As they explored the Museum site, the Ratio team realized that it should be understood as both an actual and symbolic location. The building actually occupies a footprint of perhaps 100,000 square feet of a particular section of the near-west side of downtown Indianapolis. But symbolically, given the Museum's mission, its site had to be understood as comprising the entire state.

On an even larger scale, Indiana was itself a site in the great surveyor's grid laid atop the wilderness, by the Land Ordinance of 1785 and the Northwest Ordinance of 1787. Conceived by Thomas Jefferson, this grid imposed preemptory order on the West, proclaiming it to be civilization by virtue of its imagined geometry. With statehood in 1816 came more surveyors to draw the acres and sections, townships and counties. Perhaps the state's most famous survey was the platting of Indianapolis in 1821 by Elias P. Fordham and Alexander Ralston, hired by the newborn state to come to its geographic center and then further center the state on a well-drawn capital.

Ralston had learned the art of city planning in 1791 while assisting Major Pierre Charles L'Enfant in his designs of Washington, D.C. A French architect by training, L'Enfant joined the Continental Army as an engineer and served directly under George Washington. We must believe Ralston understood L'Enfant's 1789 letter to his former commander and soon-to-be employer. "No nation," L'Enfant wrote, "perhaps had ever before the opportunity offered them of deliberately deciding on the spot where their capital city should be fixed." Substitute "state" for "nation" and the translation is complete for Indiana.

Ratio was galvanized by the deep historic meaning of this story, and took inspiration from the image of city grid within state grid within national grid – a syncopated minuet within an all-American square dance. This became the foundation of Ratio's sense of this site – with one added angle.

That angle, too, should be indirectly credited to George Washington. Spurred by his own experience as a surveyor in the wilderness, Washington would use his position as

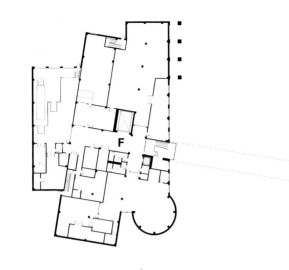

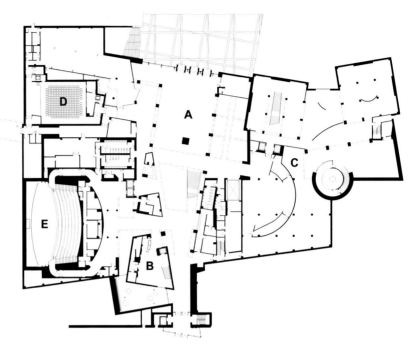

Lower Level Plan

- **A** Event Lobby
- **B** Museum Shop
- **C** Natural History Exhibits
- **D** Auditorium
- **E** IMAX Theater
- **F** Administration & Collections

N

0   20   50   100ft

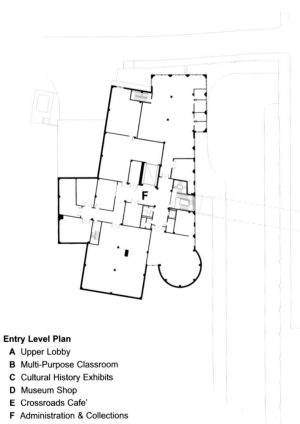

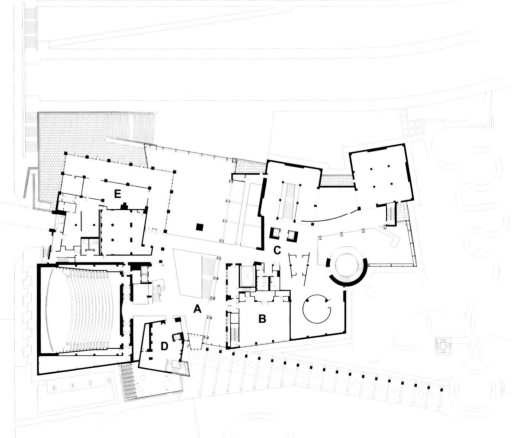

Entry Level Plan

- **A** Upper Lobby
- **B** Multi-Purpose Classroom
- **C** Cultural History Exhibits
- **D** Museum Shop
- **E** Crossroads Cafe'
- **F** Administration & Collections

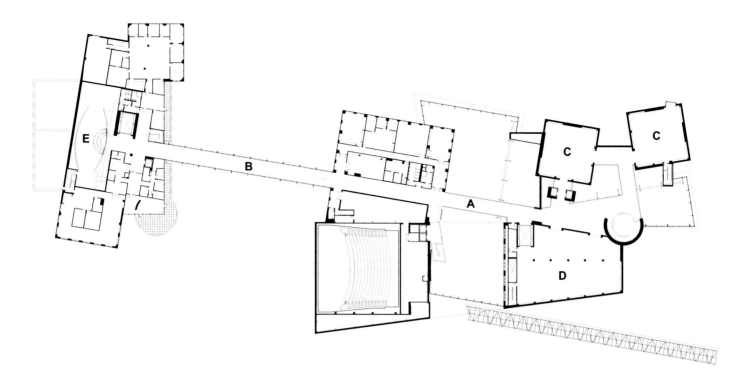

Upper Level Plan
A Bridge to Galleries
B Whipple Truss Bridge
C Art Galleries
D Changing Gallery
E Tomorrows's Indiana Gallery

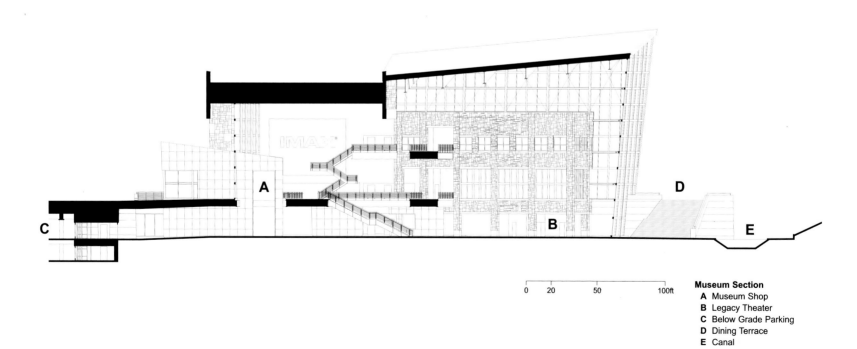

| 0 | 20 | 50 | 100ft |

Museum Section
A Museum Shop
B Legacy Theater
C Below Grade Parking
D Dining Terrace
E Canal

president to aggressively advance the idea of a National Road to link the nation's capital and the East to the burgeoning western territories. By 1827 the road had reached eastern Indiana, and its capital city three years later, flowing naturally into the city's main east-west street – known, not coincidentally, as Washington Street – then proceeding west toward the White River. In its enabling legislation the National Road was allowed to deviate slightly from its nominal straight-line progress to accommodate the most bridgeable span across rivers. When approaching the White River, surveyors determined the road required such a deviation. It was decided to bend the road

9.5 degrees to the north to best approach the river, That bend began precisely on the Museum site.

And there you have it. Browne and his team sensed this angle was the key. The longer they considered it, the more they held it up in the light, turning it this way and that in their mind's eye, the more opportunity it offered. They could see it in the patterned terrazzo of the Museum floor, where Ratio used it as the rule of a gray grid juxtaposed to the beige grid representing Ralston's. Then they took it into another dimension, using the angle to lend dramatic tilt to the north wall of the Grand Lobby and the inward slope of the gift shop's

Opposite and This Page:
The view from the southwest,
as seen in the original rendering
and photograph of the completed
structure.

As the design concept of the Indiana State Museum evolved rapidly through the summer and early autumn of 1998, the Ratio team of architects considered a wide range of strategies to make the building a living symbol of the entire state. Ratio president Bill Browne took this mission personally and literally, searching for a way to make a direct architectural connection with every Indiana visitor.

Browne had previously visited each of Indiana's 92 counties with amateur historian Doan "Buck" Wilhite and was, in a word, brimming with images and enthusiasm. He resolved it all in the idea of tangibly representing each county, from Adams to Whitley, as an artistic detail set within the exterior structure of the Museum.

Exactly how this might be accomplished was still an open question. He discussed this approach with Indianapolis designers David Young and Jeff Laramore, owners of the Young and Laramore, and 2nd Globe, a company geared to the integration of art and commerce. They responded immediately and enthusiastically, and were added to the Museum team mix. Together, Wilhite, the Ratio, and the 2nd Globe designers began contacting county officials, community foundations and historical societies, accumulating historical information and imagery and pondering the parameters of the task.

Some ground rules were clearly going to be needed. A few simple ones were immediately established. For example: All of the icons would be placed on the outside of the building; most at or near eye level, some elevated as appropriate. No representations of universities or colleges would be allowed. No representations of living persons. A more difficult decision was reached to avoid academic realism as a style of sculptural or pictorial elements; it wouldn't sit well with the architectural style of the building. Although limestone factors in 68 of the 92 county icons, the entire series also contains bronze, stainless steel, ceramics, sandstone, cast glass and others – a palette of materials as rich as the Museum's. Even more difficult was the task of distilling the cultural and historical essence of any county to a few square feet of iconography. The design team knew that almost any choice of imagery would preclude some other equally plausible choice. Would the citizens of Delaware County find sufficient meaning in an array of nine Ball jars, including the one with Garfield trapped inside? Would visitors from LaPorte County smile at the image of a limestone lighthouse? Will the folks from Parke County understand that their icon's 21 pentagonal shapes represent covered bridges? Before finalizing the design of each icon, the imagery was analyzed for the absolute accuracy of any historical reference and to ensure that no potentially controversial agendas were inadvertently presented. In the end, the design team trusted to hope that the spirit of respect and celebration integral to the 92 County Walk would communicate itself clearly. Their hope was rewarded.

For project director Susan Williams, perhaps the most significant early praise came in the form of a small gleam of light. When Williams and Browne presented the Museum design concepts to Governor Frank O'Bannon on October, 13, 1998, he was particularly taken with the idea of the 92 County Walk, presented at that point with nothing more than an oral explanation. As Williams remembered, the idea "put a twinkle in his eye" that was far more than a smile of genial approval. From that time forward, Browne said, the sense of urgency to "get this right was never in doubt."

Even before the Museum opened to the public, the 92 County Walk became its most popular feature. Construction workers would often take a few minutes at the end of the day to appraise any new icons. Since the official opening in May, 2002, that popularity has only increased in scope. Public requests for images and information about the entire series finally prompted the Museum to document the walk in a book, *The Art of the 92 County Walk*.

Left: Jeff Laramore, Mike Donham and John Brooks working on the Greene County icon at the Bybee Stone company in Elletsville.

Opposite Page: Nine of the 92 county icons. Left to Right, Top Row: Blackford, Howard, Lawrence. Second Row: Kosciusko, Marion, Scott. Third Row: Posey, Clay, Delaware.

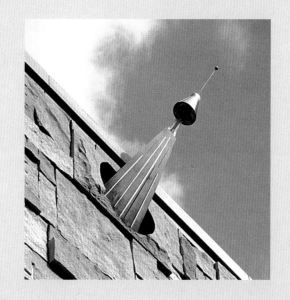

Above: The Museum's entrance canopy was inspired by the look of this overhead crane at a steel fabrication plant in Gary, the heart of Indiana's steel industry. Such structures (right) provide the basic support for industrial buildings, seen here at the Geiger and Peters plant where the Museum's major steel bents (below) were fabricated.

stainless steel walls, and finally, in the 400-foot-long avenue of the third-floor walkway as it becomes the Whipple bridge over the canal to Tomorrow's Indiana at the western end of the visitor experience. As its uses mounted, perhaps even a bit relentlessly, the angle appeared as more than just a geometric skew and somehow the perfectly "Hoosier" ingredient. It became a sidelong grin, not quite a challenge to the overall order but enough of a departure to announce the intention to literally and figuratively have their own angle on things.

The cumulative result of Ratio's use of geometry and the repeated off-angle is an edifice with a restless but somehow swelling sense of scale. Both inside and out, the building looks and feels bigger and more expansive than it is. Civilized eyes are accustomed to the normal perspective of right-angled buildings. Architectural forms grow larger or smaller in the eyes as they approach or recede. We don't think about this, we know it intuitively after years of life in a right-angled world. The Indiana State Museum plays with our visual intuition, just enough to suggest a wall or walkway might be a bit larger or farther than it actually is. The Museum's design makes that play often enough to lend the entire building a feeling of greater size than might be objectively measured, and impart a sense that the design will never quite resolve itself or settle into stability.

Browne knew that something like this would happen,

"The guys were so happy to be working on this. This project was the one you show your kids." Steve Ross, Project Manager, F. A. Wilhelm Construction

Above: Clad in stainless steel, the Museum Shop emerges from the south façade to overlook granite boulders symbolizing the ancient glacial till left when the Ice Age retreated from northern Indiana.

but admits he was surprised by the visual impact when Ratio's design was constructed. "There is no doubt that the Grand Lobby, which is already a very large space, feels like an even greater space because of the use of these angles," he said. "You can see it when you look up the main staircase, which looks to be longer and grander than its physical dimensions might suggest. And you don't so much see it as feel it when you look at the huge north wall," which leans out into the sky as it rises to its 100-foot peak. From a distance, the effect is subtle. Standing at the foot of the wall, the sensation is dramatic, as if the entire space of this vast lobby was packaged in glass and poised at the edge of an even greater space, ready to launch itself forward.

However striking its psychological effect, the off-angle created some very tangible challenges to the crews of the F. A. Wilhelm Construction Company, builders of the Museum. Like all of the nearly 300 workers employed six or even seven days a week on this very fast-track project, site bosses Steve Ross and Doug May were accustomed to building at right angles. Ratio's designs required new, sometimes unprecedented construction techniques to accommodate the demands of walls rising from floors at 80.5-degree or 99.5-degree angles, depending on how you looked at it, or of panes of glass that had to be cut as trapezoids rather than rectangles. Telling their stories of the Museum construction, Ross and May at times just laugh, rather than attempt to explain.

May remembered bringing his future wife to the construction site soon after the odd-angled, stainless steel shell of the Museum store had been built, appearing to pierce the main south wall. "She took one look and said, 'Oh my God, honey, what happened?' "

The pervasive use of these 9.5 degrees – as well as subtle variations that Ratio devised for aesthetic effect or structural necessity – was not the last of the Wilhelm company's challenges. Because the Museum was designed as a series of almost independent boxed spaces inside a larger container, the entire construction schedule was a highly unusual mix of isolated projects within a larger project, resembling at points either a jigsaw puzzle or an intricately choreographed ballet. Such challenges are the price of special projects, but also the reward. As Ross said, "The guys were so happy to be working on this. This project was the one you show your kids." Almost two years after completion, May still drives out of his way just to pass near the Museum, even if just for a distant glance.

Williams smiles at such anecdotes and is quick to follow them with others, stories of workers going the extra distance, of doing whatever it took to get it right. She remembers the brick masons going to extraordinary lengths to perfectly align the bricks of the huge cylinder surrounding the Foucault pendulum, of workers staying after the five o'clock whistle just to stroll the site to inspect that day's progress – something she had never seen before. "As I was walking around one Friday, one of the guys – he didn't give his name and I didn't ask – stopped me and said, 'You are really doing something special here. This building really means something.' I think I will remember that for the rest of my life."

*This view from the
Administration Building
shows the intricate structural
detailing on the Whipple Truss
Bridge and highlights the variety
of colors in the sandstone wall.*

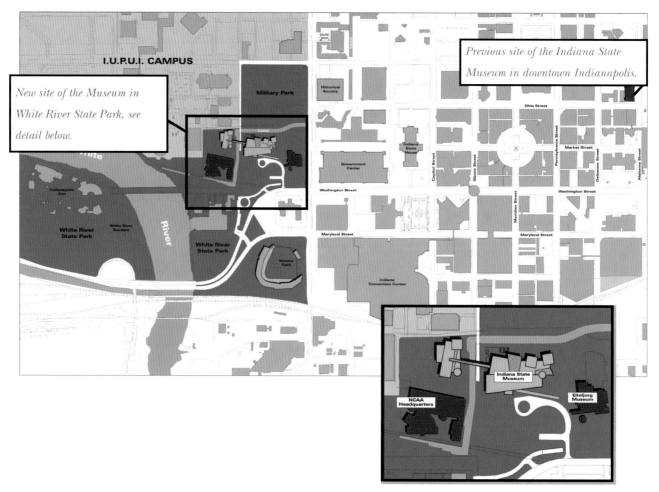

New site of the Museum in White River State Park, see detail below.

Previous site of the Indiana State Museum in downtown Indianapolis.

Context Plan

long with the regular grid and the Hoosier-skew off-angle, the Museum site offered the architects another dichotomy: equal alignment with urban and pastoral contexts. East and west, it fit snugly within downtown Indianapolis. South and north, the Museum faced sprawling parkland – the great south lawn, part of the artful landscaping leading down to the river, and on the north, historical Camp Sullivan Military Park. Which context should the museum honor most? Again, in keeping with the comings and goings of the Hoosier spirit, the answer was both.

Rob Proctor, second in charge of the Ratio design team, remem-bered this dilemma as a critical creative tension in the summer of 1998, resolved in the idea of a building with two distinct facades. Although hardly the textbook approach, the idea seemed war-ranted, even demanded by the site. "We conceived of the south wall as a garden wall, but at a far greater scale because of the size of the lawn in front of it and because it would always be seen from a distance as people drove up to the Museum," Proctor explained. "But the north façade along the canal could only be approached by pedestrians, which is a typical urban way of experiencing architecture. We began to think of the south wall as the closed, conservative side of Indiana – literally stony-faced – and the north as the jaunty, urban character." It all fit: fac-

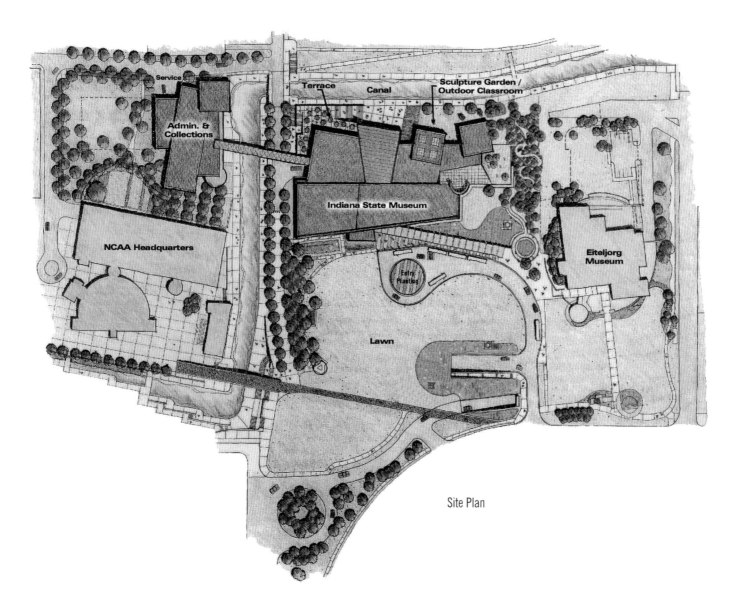

Site Plan

ing the rural, stone-laced southern half of the state with a stone façade, and facing the steel-and-glass northern half of the Indiana with just those materials.

Each of the two facades would necessarily offer a separate entrance. The south façade's would be grand and public, used primarily by school buses and tour groups. Seizing the opportunity to incorporate function and symbolism in the same structural element, the Ratio team designed a 19-bay canopy to shelter visitors and remind them through sidewalk inlays of Indiana's position as the 19th state. The Museum's north façade would be scaled to an urban streetscape. The Museum would also require a major entrance from the underground park-

ing garage. Ratio anticipated this would be primary entrance for perhaps three-quarters of all Museum visitors. "We worked very, very hard," Proctor said, "to make that entrance a strong, important statement." The Ratio team squeezed every possible inch of vertical space into the plan, and looked for any conceivable way to bring sunlight into that passageway. Browne said the breakthrough came when the team realized there was a gap of over 20 feet between the south wall of the IMAX foundation and the north wall of the garage. "Why the original planners did that is a mystery," Browne said. "But it gave us a chance to open it up to the sky and create the waterfall and pool to give that entrance a graceful identity."

The vertical circulation through the Museum's three floors would become a pilgrimage through time and through the three tiers of the Museum's mission: natural history, cultural history and art.

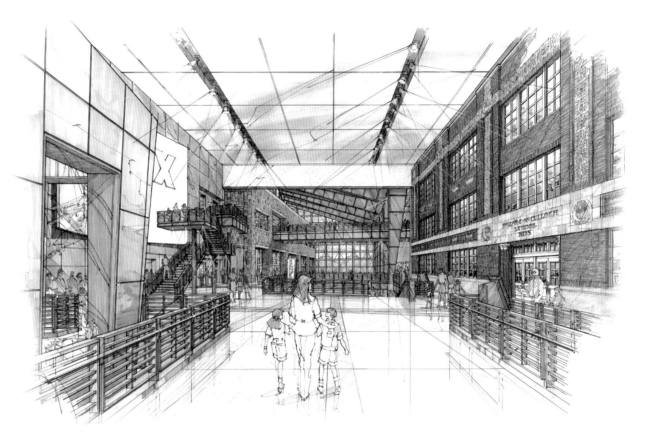

A similar opportunity to offer grace and symbolic meaning presented itself to the east of the Museum, in the landscaped space visible through the virtual quarry window wall. That space is punctuated by fractured or rust stained limestone blocks which might be found at the edge of a working quarry, thus completing the simulation inside. The Ratio team extended the narrative even further by locating these blocks within a garden metaphor of Indiana, incorporating native species of plant material, from trees to prairie grasses and wildflowers, and including a meandering pathway to suggest a slowly winding Hoosier river. Crediting Ratio landscape architect John Jackson, Browne anticipates a fulfilled landscape vision when the larger shade trees reach early maturity in a few years. With the canal bordering the Museum and its neighbor to the west, this garden provides an equally graceful transition to its neighbor on the east.

Those neighbors played an intrinsic part in Ratio's design considerations. By the time Ratio took over in 1998, the Museum site had two immediate neighbors, the existing Eiteljorg Museum to the east and, on its west, the new headquarters of the National Collegiate Athletic Association designed (but not yet built) by Indianapolis-born, internationally acclaimed architect Michael Graves. The NCAA included its Hall of Champions, a museum of college athletics. Both neighbors were first-rate designs, both demonstrated strong historical influences. The Indiana State Museum would be the public centerpiece between these two private institutions, by far the largest and, for the citizenry the most significant statement.

Below: An illustration, a computer rendering and a photograph of the Museum's Foucault Pendulum. The pendulum was purchased and installed by Museum Director R. D. Starrett in the late 1960s as a signature element for the facility at 202 North Alabama. Its ongoing popularity made its presence in the new building mandatory.

Opposite Page: An original design rendering of the Grand Lobby as seen from the main entrance.

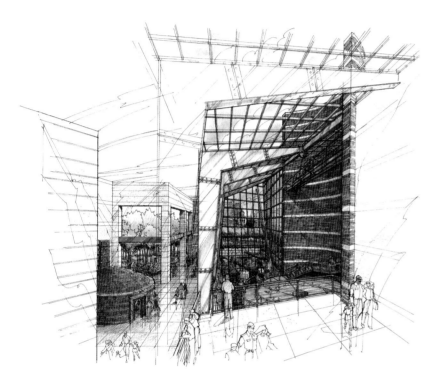

Left Page: The Museum's Foucault Pendulum swings through its daily rounds in a towering brick cylinder designed specifically to house this visitor favorite.

Clockwise, From Upper Left: The Museum Shop offers two floors of Indiana art, artifacts and mementos.

Beneath the Foucault pendulum and the towering brick cylinder that houses it, the Museum has created a naturalist's laboratory for visitors young and old to explore the wonders of paleontology.

The full panorama of Indiana's cultural and natural history can be surveyed through the vertical vista created by the open design of the Museum's exhibition wing.

The lowest of the Museum's three exhibition floors represents the deepest layers of Indiana history, the ancient oceanic life that over the eons formed the limestone bedrock of the state.

Below: The eastern view of the Museum at sunrise, overlooking the abandoned quarry blocks. Opposite Page: A chronological sequence of construction detailing the 24-month process of building the Museum.

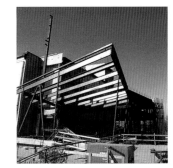

If complementing two immediate neighbors in White River State Park presented a challenge, Ratio realized they must also position the Indiana State Museum in the larger national and international context of museum design. Only by succeeding in those arenas would the design truly fulfill its mission.

As Proctor remembered, the Ratio team addressed this challenge directly, asking themselves, "Well, what should a museum look like? It took some reading and some thinking and looking and we realized some very simple attributes of most modern museums. First, they looked solid, with not a lot of windows. Second, they had a strong statement of a front door." The Eiteljorg Museum had used this basic formula to great effect, and Ratio decided it could capture some of the same strength of simplicity at a larger, grander scale if counterpointed by other textures and volumes.

Corollary ideas grew out of the team's visit to the J. Paul Getty Museum, with its collection of freestanding pavilions perched atop a foothill overlooking Los Angeles. After experiencing the visual dynamic of the Getty, with its near and distant views, Browne realized that the Indiana State Museum might offer a similar visual dialogue. The Ratio team set about planning the sightlines from the elevated walkways traversing the Grand Lobby, counterpointing the contained view to the north through the trees of Military Park with the far industrial horizon seen to the south, rising over the Museum's green lawn.

The second strong idea that Browne distilled from the Getty was to envision the Grand Lobby, the main public space of the Museum, as a courtyard bordered by the façades of almost independent structures. This approach immediately solved the dilemma of where to put the demolished School #5 exterior: in the Museum's interior, as Ratio had first suggested 15 years before. Thus another layer was added to the Museum's

evolving ballet of meanings. Now inside and outside were dancing around each other. Complementing the brick and terra cotta façade of School #5 was the stainless steel module of the Museum gift shop, the sandstone façade of the northwest pavilion, the huge glass treasure cases that signaled the entrance to the permanent exhibition quadrant to the east, and the IMAX entrance to the southwest. Set just enough off parallel to save the lobby from predictability, the façades of these main quadrants keep the viewer's gaze restless, energized. As the team began fitting the pieces together, it realized how smoothly this approach paralleled the necessity of the lobby's three entrances.

The design process was picking up momentum. Each successful decision suggested another, then together yet another. Causes were becoming effects, which in turn suggested other causes for design decisions. The visitor's visual and physical passage on the Museum's main north-south axis cried out for an equal east-west corridor, now supplied by the twin spans of the Whipple Truss Bridge and the elevated walkway to the third-floor galleries. With these two axes established, it was now obvious that the Museum required equally dramatic vertical circulation, at first visually and then, as the idea really took root, conceptually. The vertical circulation through the Museum's three floors would become a pilgrimage through time and through the three tiers of the Museum's mission: natural history, cultural history and art. Again, how perfect: The Foucault Pendulum, perhaps the best known, most popular souvenir of the old Museum on North Alabama Street, needed a great vertical space.

And this decision only seemed to reinforce the rapidly evolving consensus that the Museum's three distinct missions could be presented dynamically, yet intelligibly on its three distinct levels. The ground floor would speak to Indiana's nat-

Indiana's role as the Crossroads of America is echoed in the flow and crisscross of the Museum's bridges and walkways.

Proctor likened the accelerating design process to assembling
a jigsaw puzzle, with progress made haltingly at first,
but faster and faster as the bigger picture comes into focus.

ural history and be closest to the site itself. The second floor
would tell the story of the material culture, of the things we
made and the people who made them. And the third floor
would present Indiana's art and aspirations, its character and
metaphors, the visions that become our goals. And from
there, the Museum would lead us onward and westward, over
the bridge to Tomorrow's Indiana.

Proctor likened the accelerating design process to assembling a jigsaw puzzle, with progress made haltingly at first, but
faster and faster as the bigger picture comes into focus. This
cascade of decisions propelled the team and taught them a
sense of confidence born of necessity, Proctor said. Without
time to debate, ponder and mull, the architects grew the collective ability to decide quickly and to trust their decisions.
For Browne and Proctor the day began at 6 a.m., reviewing
yesterday's progress, setting today's agenda, anticipating
tomorrow. The necessity of time became the mother not just
of invention but also of confidence.

Browne summed it up this way: "I am convinced that if we
had won the contract initially, if we had been designing the
Museum a year earlier and working slowly, carefully through
a more normal process, that the design would never have evolved
this way – and never been this good.

"We would have been more cautious and taken fewer
chances in our designs. We would never have dared some of
the things we did and would have probably been always looking over our shoulders or looking around for approval. And
we never would have developed the confidence to believe that
our intuitions were strong enough to follow. It would have been
a safer, maybe more tastefully 'correct' design. And it would
not have told the same story with the same force or spirit."

*The north façade as seen from
Military Park at dusk.*

In the fall of 1998, as the Ratio team of designers reached the end of the thematic development and design of the building, it was time to identify a designer for the permanent exhibits. The team quickly focused its attention on Ralph Appelbaum Associates (RAA) and just as quickly brought them aboard. RAA describes itself as the largest interpretative design firm in the world, with more than 75 specialists in all aspects of exhibition design and communication. Based in New York and London, the firm is just-ly famous for its exhibit work in muse-ums as diverse as the United States Memorial Holocaust Museum in Washington, D.C.; the Country Music Hall of Fame and Museum in Nashville, TN; the renovated dinosaur halls in the American Museum of Natural History in New York City; the Harley-Davidson Museum and Rider Center in Milwaukee; the National Museum of Prehistory in Taiwan; and the Salvation Army Visitor's Center in London. In short, the firm's range was every bit as encyclopedic as Ratio's sense of Indiana, and the two firms seemed to propel each other's perceptions of the meaning of Hoosier spirit and the Museum's mission.

The RAA team immediately under-stood and took to heart the oppor-tunities that Ratio had given them

with its three-level concept of an exhibition space progressing up from the prehistoric and geological to the cultural to the artistic. Appelbaum praised "the view corridors" Ratio designed through the building. These generated "real visual excitement not just with the layered views of history but also the views of the capitol and the panoramas out the windows. This allowed us to open up the Museum experience, in a sense turning the story inside out, to see the fullness of the state in dialogue with the exhibition, to allow the visitor experience and the story to become one."

And perhaps even most important, RAA immediately established a sense of common cause with the Museum staff, building a mutually enlighten-ing dialogue. RAA knew exhibit design like nobody's business; the Museum staff knew Indiana just as well. This collaborative spirit stood in marked contrast to the working process the staff had experienced with the designers from Gerard Hilferty and Associates, an Ohio-based exhibition design firm that had been part of the original team but had left the proj-ect shortly after the transition of architects.

Together, RAA and the staff realized the need to find fundamental and unifying themes within the great scope of their subject. As Museum cura-tor Jim May explained it, "We had 4.6 billion years of Indiana history to explain in a little more than 55,000 square feet of exhibition space. Although this was three times the space we had in the old Museum, it still required a great deal of creativity and some tough calls to design a coher-ent progression of stories. In the old building because of its design, we were only able to tell a series of disconnected small stories, but occa-sionally tell them with some depth. The new building design allowed us

The Museum's collection is presented through a variety of media and techniques, offering opportunities to interact, to discover, to reminisce, and to wonder.

to tell one very long epic story that would wind through three floors."

Armed with Ratio's persuasive analysis of the Hoosier character, immersed in the staff's expertise and observations, made concrete by trips around the state, Appelbaum and his colleagues were soon speaking of the embedded stories of continuity and contradiction, tradition and innovation, connection and independence, of family and individualism. "We realized there really was a special spirit about this state and this project, and we responded to it," Appelbaum said. "There is something about Indiana that speaks to the whole American character, not just as Hoosiers. Our team was discovering stories of who we are in this almost perfect heartland."

Yet despite the range of the team's perceptions and their overarching sense of Hoosier pride, Appelbaum also had a sense that "Indiana has been challenged for many years to update its image and take its rightful position as a powerful creative contributor to the national culture. We very much wanted the Museum to be a reflection of that grand aspiration. We wanted the Museum and its exhibitions to be an armature for the future."

And to that end, Appelbaum made a powerful suggestion to Williams and Browne. Instead of using the western pavilion merely as an administration building, create a gallery space there and let Museum visitors walk the Whipple Truss Bridge over the canal in a symbolic pilgrimage west to the future, as Americans have always done. It was a brilliant idea that summed up the spirit of the architecture and completed it. And thus was born "Tomorrow's Indiana," the capstone of Hoosier history, its view and vote to the future.

The core of Appelbaum's concept of the Museum was the three-tiered vision and division of Indiana's story. The exhibition evolves as it rises: up from ancient prehistory of the ground floor, through the industrial and cultural history on the second floor, culminating in the third floor's art gallery.

CELEBRATING INDIANA

In the fall of 1996, the Indiana State Museum Society, (later to be named Indiana State Museum Foundation) asked long-time museum professional Ron Newlin to start a statewide dialogue about the idea of a new Museum. The society realized that a new Museum required not just a financial investment, but an emotional, intellectual and, in the largest sense of the word, a civic investment from the people of Indiana. More than a cabinet of wonders worth a visit when next in Indianapolis, the new Museum must be seen as a magnifying mirror to reflect and enlarge what the people brought to it.

Newlin arranged 20 meetings, two each in 10 Indiana cities, to brainstorm with community leaders and opinion makers. Many ideas for Museum content or form were generated, some predictably local in scope, others surprisingly broad in their appeal. When asked what Indiana theme best suited an "immersive" exhibit, that is, an exhibit that replicated a real-world environment inside the museum, 19 of 20 meetings asked for a limestone quarry. (That request made its way to the finished Museum.) When the ideas overflowed, Newlin would re-focus the conversation with a deceptively simple question: "Why build a new Indiana State Museum?"

As obvious as it may sound, that catalyzing question revealed any number of other questions within it: Why build it now? What about Indiana needs a bigger and better showcase? What stories should the Museum tell first, second or later? What do we hope the Museum will accomplish?

At the end of the three-month process, the fundamental answer to that fundamental question was clear: Why build a new Indiana State Museum? To make us proud. Indeed, that answer was spoken with enough force to be an imperative, a command from the local communities to the Museum planners: "Make us proud."

In the past, pride may have been assumed. Traditionally this question would have been answered, "Make us proud" without hesitation. But modern museums are different and such answers less certain, and the planners heard an underlying message. When the people of Indiana said they wanted a museum to embody pride, it was because, perhaps, they felt its absence.

There was a time when Indiana was to America what America was to the world. There was a time when Indiana was vital and a little wild, slow and solid as Southern stone, sharp and changeable as Northern steel, old-fashioned yet inventive, practical yet idealistic. In 1919, when Hoosier journalist William Herschell poetically asked "Ain't God good to Indiana?" there was a legion of reasons to answer in the affirmative. Economically, culturally, artistically, politically, Indiana was a major center of national gravity. But as the 20th century came to a close, celestial favor felt less certain. Instead of assuming, Hoosiers now asked, "Did the state have the right stuff to make its way in the new era?"

Perhaps this question signaled lack of confidence. Or perhaps it grew from the courage to ask the hard questions – and not retreat into a reflex recitation of graces to the state. As Newlin heard it, the people in his meetings wanted the Museum to tell the whole story of Indiana in a way that gave us the courage and confidence to ask any question and deal with any answer.

This was the challenge presented and the challenge fulfilled: To build an Indiana State Museum that both informs and inspires, that literally gives true form to Hoosier history and equally gives pride and spirit to Indiana's future. This

The Museum's traditional New Year's Eve celebration, an annual event designed for Hoosier families, seen here ringing in New Year's 2003.

When Ratio Architects began evaluating the Museum site, they made the unpleasant discovery that a major steam line owned by Indianapolis Power and Light (IPL) ran beneath it. This was more than inconvenient, it was crippling. Any major construction would require an expensive relocation of several hundred feet of line.

Although necessary, the decision left project leader Susan Williams feeling a bit steamed, if you will — mad at whatever park administrator had blithely approved this placement years ago with no regard for the future Museum; mad at the injustice of inherited problems. She was determined to somehow turn the situation to the Museum's admittedly expensive advantage.

As the relocation project progressed, an IPL executive remarked to Williams that he had recently seen and heard a marvelous steam clock on a visit to Vancouver. Seizing this idea as the antidote to her steamline blues, Williams contacted the designer, a septuagenarian horologist named Ray Saunders. With a little bit of coaxing, Saunders accepted the commission to design a modern steam whistle clock that would play a distinctive Hoosier tune. The obvious choice, was "Back Home Again in Indiana," the 1917 ballad by James F. Hanley with words by Ballard MacDonald. The signature melody of the opening line, matching notes to syllables of the title line, required eight notes. Michael Runyan, a friend of Williams at the Indianapolis Symphony Orchestra, recorded several versions of the tune and emailed them to Saunders, who successfully conducted his computerized equipment to produce the perfect whistles.

The Indiana Steam Clock now whistles its Hoosier heart out every 15 minutes, thanks to a generous donation from Bill and Nancy Hunt

of Columbus, IN. Depending on the stillness of the day, its tune may be heard over a mile away, throughout the IUPUI campus on the north and into the center of downtown Indianapolis if the wind is blowing in the right direction. Its mood is undeniably cheery, literally lending a recurring note of festivity to the Museum, forever reminding us of the essential purpose of the institution. As Williams said, "The clock calls us to the celebration."

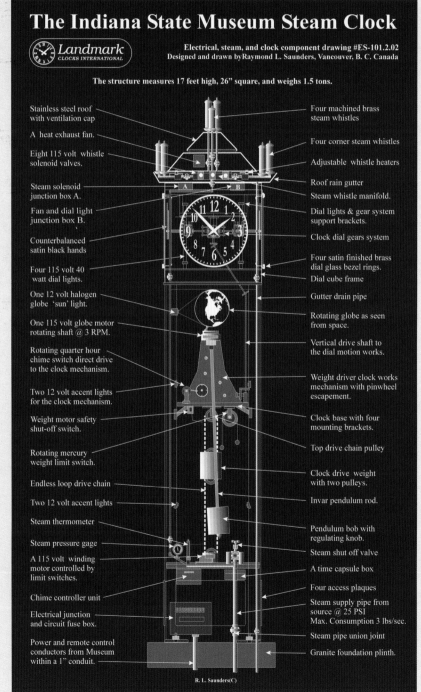

The Indiana State Museum Steam Clock

Landmark CLOCKS INTERNATIONAL

Electrical, steam, and clock component drawing #ES-101.2.02
Designed and drawn by Raymond L. Saunders, Vancouver, B. C. Canada

The structure measures 17 feet high, 26" square, and weighs 1.5 tons.

Stainless steel roof with ventilation cap
A heat exhaust fan.
Eight 115 volt whistle solenoid valves.
Steam solenoid junction box A.
Fan and dial light junction box B.
Counterbalanced satin black hands
Four 115 volt 40 watt dial lights.
One 12 volt halogen globe 'sun' light.
One 115 volt globe motor rotating shaft @ 3 RPM.
Rotating quarter hour chime switch direct drive to the clock mechanism.
Two 12 volt accent lights for the clock mechanism.
Weight motor safety shut-off switch.
Rotating mercury weight limit switch.
Endless loop drive chain
Two 12 volt accent lights
Steam thermometer
Steam pressure gage
A 115 volt winding motor controlled by limit switches.
Chime controller unit
Electrical junction and circuit fuse box.
Power and remote control conductors from Museum within a 1" conduit.

Four machined brass steam whistles
Four corner steam whistles
Adjustable whistle heaters
Roof rain gutter
Steam whistle manifold.
Dial lights & gear system support brackets.
Clock dial gears system
Four satin finished brass dial glass bezel rings.
Dial cube frame
Gutter drain pipe
Rotating globe as seen from space.
Vertical drive shaft to the dial motion works.
Weight driver clock works mechanism with pinwheel escapement.
Clock base with four mounting brackets.
Top drive chain pulley
Clock drive weight with two pulleys.
Invar pendulum rod.
Pendulum bob with regulating knob.
Steam shut off valve
A time capsule box
Four access plaques
Steam supply pipe from source @ 25 PSI Max. Consumption 3 lbs/sec.
Steam pipe union joint
Granite foundation plinth.

R. L. Saunders(C)

Horologist Ray Saunders at work installing his creation, enthusiastically assisted by a young man with time on his hands, Keegan Browne.
Left: Horologist Ray Saunders' blueprint of the Hoosier Steam Clock.

Indeed, that answer was spoken with enough force to be an imperative, a command
from the local communities to the Museum planners: "Make us proud."

is no simple task. Information and inspiration do not readily harmonize even in words. Even more difficult was to
embody them in stone and steel

Yet at its best, architecture can give unity to even the most
paradoxical mission, can reconcile fact to aspiration. Indeed,
when a design resolves and transcends this tension, its physical form becomes, perhaps ironically, proof that any appar-
ent paradox is actually a partnership. The house creates the
marriage.

The institution was ready to accept the challenge, ready
to assume responsibility for its new home. As Dale Ogden,
the Museum's curator of cultural materials, explained it,
"It is important to understand that the Indiana State
Museum didn't just move. We closed the old building and,
in a sense, the old idea of what we were." In the process,
Ogden said, "We learned a certain kind of courage. In one
sense this meant not being defensive about who and what
we were as a state, about not underselling the image of a bas-
ketball bouncing in a corn field because it had been done
a thousand times before or because we were hesitant to appear
too much the hick. In another sense, it was the courage to
honestly and objectively talk about some of the painful and
unfortunate aspects of Indiana history. Being in the new Museum
has given us that courage. When the decision was made to
display the Ku Klux Klan uniform in the opening exhibition,
I kept waiting for the call to tell me to take it out. That call
never came. We are proud of that silence."

With this new courage and confidence, Ogden believes
the Museum staff will dream bigger dreams – and convince
others to dream along with them. "Although the new
Museum gives us vast opportunity to display the collection
to a much greater extent – and we probably have upwards

*Above: Groundbreaking on
August 30, 1999. In their
enthusiasm, these school children
scattered their shovelfuls of good
Hoosier dirt with gleeful abandon,
surprising the Governor and
First Lady.*
*Left: Each in his own way, these
three Indiana governors advanced
the dream of a new State Museum
in White River State Park. Left to
right, Otis Bowen, Frank
O'Bannon and Robert Orr.*

An amateur photographer, Gov. Frank O'Bannon captured this image of the Indiana State Museum and the White River State Park while returning via helicopter to the Statehouse.

A view through three floors, the full spectrum of the Museum's themes: from art at the top, through the vast sweep of Indiana's cultural and industrial history, and down to its ancient bedrock, glimpsed past the steel column at the right edge of the view.

of 400,000 artifacts, counting every shrew's knuckle in storage – the institution has really outgrown its collection. For a state museum of this size and potential, we have too few artifacts capable of eliciting a 'Holy cow! Look at that!' from the visitors. For the time being," Ogden said, "that 'Holy cow!' is being generated by the architecture. The building is carrying us forward now. That's a compliment but also quite a challenge. As an institution, we will need to catch up with the building. We will need to live up to the architecture."

As Susan Williams remembered, this was exactly what Gov. O'Bannon knew the Indiana State Museum should and could provide. "The Governor had a deep philosophical belief," Williams said, "that if we celebrated our cultural heritage in the right way, in the right building, it would give us the pride and the strength we would need in the future."

After her husband's death, Mrs. Judy O'Bannon amplified Williams' recollection with her own analysis: "Frank and I always knew that Indiana could be more, and the Museum could be the thing that raises our vision of ourselves."

"Maybe it was his experience growing up in Corydon with the old State Capitol just across the street," Mrs. O'Bannon recalled, "and his understanding of how a building like that can be the focal point of the community, how it brought people together and meant so much to so many different people. Frank always felt that the Indiana State Museum could be that for the whole state," by being, she said, "a challenge and charge. And I think you can feel that in this Museum. You can feel it reaching up to the sky."

As the architects developed the idea and design of the Museum's Grand Lobby, it became increasingly important to find some major signature element to punctuate but not dominate its vast space. Ralph Appelbaum suggested a number of ideas, including a great globe with electronic displays that would scroll through every name in every Indiana phone book – a marvelous but ultimately unfeasible concept. Finally Appelbaum suggested the perfect signature statement for the Indiana State Museum might be just that: a signature of the state by the state's native son self-named for the state – a giant INDIANA by Robert Indiana. It would be called the INDIANA Obelisk and measure 49-feet in height.

Seemingly a simple idea, it created more consternation than nearly any other element in the Museum design and construction, most of it generated by the artist. Notoriously unconcerned by other people's schedules or, for that matter, his own, artist Indiana lived up to his reputation and tested Susan Williams' patience to the point of exasperation. It started at the beginning. When the decision was made in March, 1999 to commission the sculpture, the Governor sent an effusive letter requesting Indiana's participation in this great undertaking. It went unanswered for weeks. When Williams and Browne had to visit the artist on his New England island retreat, it took more weeks to confirm the date of their trip. When he came to Indianapolis in April, 2002 to be honored and to thank all those who had supported the cause (particularly Polly Horton Hix, who underwrote the piece for

Left: Native son artist Robert Indiana atop one element of his INDIANA Obelisk at Milgo's Industrial Fabrication shop in Brooklyn, NY. Below: the Obelisk was delivered by truck in two sections for final assembly atop its' 7 foot granite base.

$750,000), there was always the worry he would disappear to who knows where. Yet in the end he delivered, not only the sculpture but himself. He managed to attend every ceremony and reception in his honor – thanks in part to the threat of an escort of state troopers Williams could arrange for his, ah, convenience. Unabashed by any tension during the three-year process, Indiana requested one last consideration: that a tomb be constructed beneath his sculpture, a final resting place for the man who created this monument. This idea was politely rejected by project leadership with only a trace of a smile.

Standing proudly, the towering INDIANA Obelisk declares its identity and origin, centering the Museum at the Crossroads of America.

Opposite Page: The waterfall in winter, a frozen poem of light and water, stone and steel — a moment of beauty built of "leftover" space discovered empty between the Museum's original footprint and the subterranean parking garage.

Left: The Administration Building is both connected and separate from the main Museum. It completes the implied western migration of the visitor's experience, across the bridge and into the future.

Below: The east wing at dusk. The Museum's quarry exhibit turns inside out as the days shadows become evenings highlights.

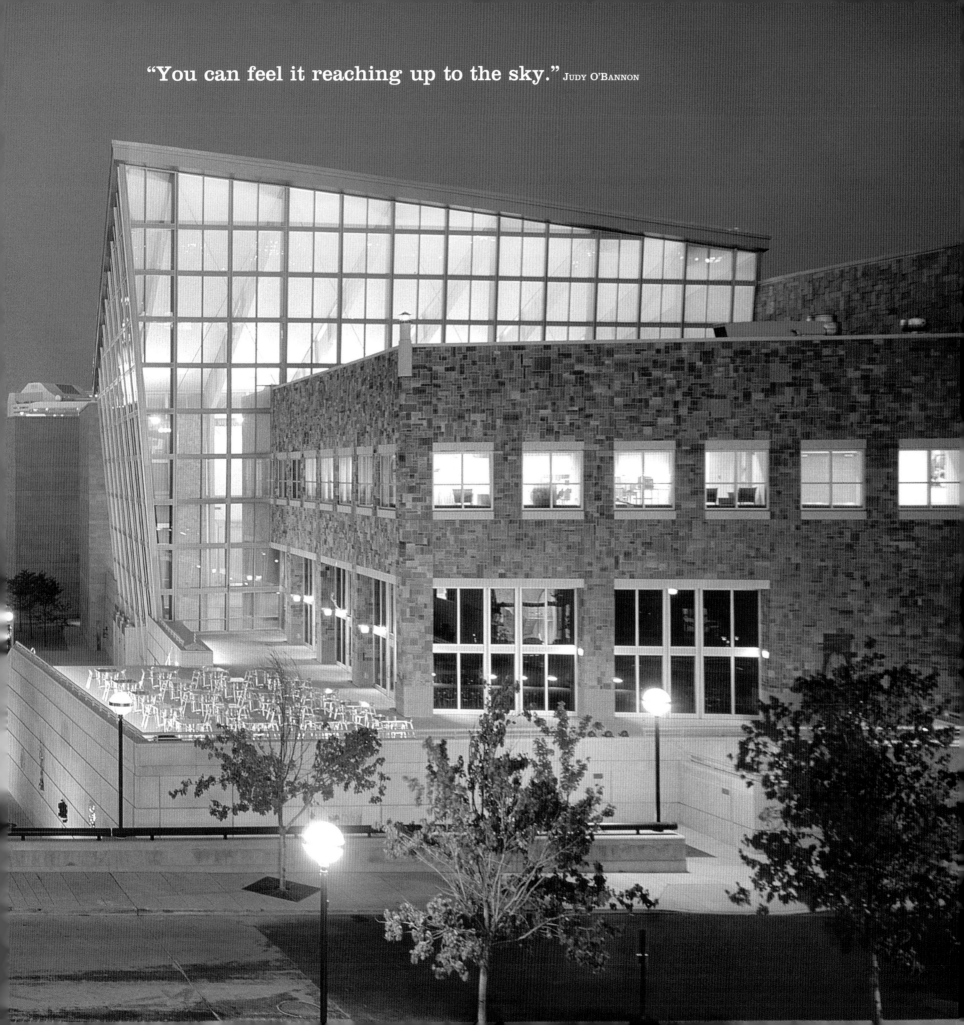

"You can feel it reaching up to the sky." JUDY O'BANNON

"The Governor had a deep philosophical belief," Williams remembered, "that if we celebrated our cultural heritage in the right way, in the right building, it would give us the pride and the strength we would need in the future."

Fun Facts at the Indiana State Museum

1. **Construction Duration**
   995 days from ground breaking to ribbon cutting
2. **Length of South Wall** 334 feet
3. **Height of South Wall** 64 feet 4 inches
   at the main entrance
4. **Height of North Lobby Wall**
   104 feet 4 inches at its peak
5. **Height of Tapered Brick Cylinder** 109 feet
6. **Height of INDIANA Obelisk** 49 feet
   6 feet x 6 feet Letters with a 7 feet cube base
7. **Height of Indiana Steam Clock** 17 feet
8. **Width/Height of School 5 Façade**
   83 feet, 8 inches x 46 feet, 6 inches
9. **Museum Building Size**
   187,000 gross square feet
10. **Administration Building Size**
    97,000 gross square feet
11. **Cubic Volume of Grand Lobby**
    1,300,000 cubic feet
12. **Whipple Truss Bridge Span** 175 feet
13. **Weight of Entrance Concrete Lintel**
    120,000 pounds of poured-in-place concrete
14. **Length of Foucault Pendulum** 60 feet
15. **Types of Indiana Limestone:**
    South Wall: Variegated Roughbacks
    East Pavilion Cube: Smooth Buff Select
       with Rustic Buff Banding
    West Pavilion Cube: Smooth Variegated
       with Rustic Buff Banding
    Administration Cube: Smooth Variegated
       with Buff Banding

16. **Types of Granite:**
    Limestone Base: Oconee Buff (Georgia)
    Sandstone Base: Golden Leaf (Saudia Arabia)
    Stainless Steel Base: Mesabi (Minnesota)
17. **Species of Wood Veneer**
    American Sycamore
18. **Number of Stainless Steel Panels**
    792 panels
19. **Number of Bricks** 350,000 bricks
20. **Number of Smooth Limestone Pieces**
    8,000 pieces
21. **Weight of Roughback Limestone**
    2,200,000 pounds
22. **Weight of Indiana Sandstone**
    1,100,000 pounds
23. **Number of Granite Pieces**
    1,500 pieces
24. **Weight of Steel** 5,200,000 pounds
25. **Weight of Largest Glacial Till Granite Boulder**
    (in fountain) 80,000 pounds
26. **Number of Terrazzo Stair Steps**
    349 steps
27. **Number of Artists/Artisans in 92 County Walk**
    32
28. **Number of Feet of Wiring**
    558,534 feet
29. **Building Construction Cost**
    $65,000,000
30. **Permanent Exhibit Cost**
    $40,000,000
31. **School 5 Bell Cost** $35.00 on EBay

BOOK DONORS:

The Indiana State Museum Foundation is grateful to the following project partners whose generous donations made the publication of this book possible:

Ratio Architects
Circle Design Group
Evans Limestone
Fink, Roberts & Petrie
F.A. Wilhelm Construction Co.
The Shaheen Family
Geiger & Peters
Paul I. Cripe
American Consulting Engineers
Blakley Corporation

MUSEUM PROJECT TEAM

Susan Williams, *Executive Director, Indiana State Office Building Commission*

Bob Wilson, *Deputy Director, Indiana State Office Building Commission*

Larry Macklin, *Director, Indiana Department of Natural Resources*

D.J. Sigler, *Exec. Assist. Special Projects, Indiana Department of Natural Resources*

Sheila Snider, *FAIA, Director of Public Works, Indiana Department of Administration*

Joyce Martin, *Office of the Governor*

Jeff Myers, *Assistant Director for Operations, Indiana State Museum*

Jim May, *Manager of Collections, Indiana State Museum*

Kathleen McLary, *Director of Programs, Indiana State Museum*

Lee Alig, *Indiana State Museum Trustee*

Kent Agness, *Indiana State Museum Foundation*

Doug Wade, *Indiana State Museum Foundation*

Tom Castaldi, *Indiana State Museum Foundation*

Paula Lopossa, *Indiana State Museum Foundation*

Ron Newlin, *Executive Director, Indiana State Museum Foundation*

William Browne, Jr., *Principal Architect, Ratio Architects*

John Klipsch, *Project Manager, Klipsch Consulting, LLC*

DESIGN TEAM

Ratio Architects, Architect:

William Browne, Jr., *AIA, Principal Architect*

Rob Proctor, Jr., *AIA, Design Architect*

John Hartlep, *AIA, Project Director*

Bryan Strube, *Project Architect*

Ratio Design Team Members:

Ken Boyce, Jennifer Broemel, Tony Brummett, Ivette Bruns, Larry George, Brett Hatchett, John Jackson, Connie Jung, David Kroll, Gerard Lehner, Michele Meregaglia, Adam Ratcliff, Drew Risch, Steve Risting, Frank Rocchio, Rob Rosner, Sean Sanger, Chuck Scarbrough, Leonard Scheurich, Rebecca Thompson, Jason Victor, Dan Wurst *(deceased)*

Fink Roberts & Petrie, *Structural Engineer*

Michael Natali, *Principal Engineer*

Scott Rouse, *Project Engineer*

Circle Design Group, *Mechanical/Electrical Engineer*

Kerry Smith, *Principal Mechanical Engineer*

Jeff Wiley, *Principal Electrical Engineer*

American Consulting Engineers, *Civil Engineer*

Alen Fetahagic, *Project Manager*

Jeff Clayton, *Project Manager*

Fisher Marantz, Renfro Stone, *Lighting Designer*

Jaffe Holden, Scarbrough Acoustics, *Acoustic Designer*

RLR Associates, *Environmental Graphic Designer*

Fehribach Group, *Inclusive Design and Access Consultant*

Gregory Fehribach, *Attorney at Law*

Ralph Applebaum Associates, *Permanent Exhibit Designer*

2nd Globe Sculptures, *92 County Walk Designer*

Midwest Model Makers, *Building Model Fabricator*

Paul I. Cripe, *Owner's Technical Representative*

Don Currise, *Project Manager*

Pat Taylor, *Field Coordinator*

Frank Obie III, *GM Construction, Cost Estimator*

CONSTRUCTION TEAM

F.A. Wilhelm Construction Co., *General Contractor*

Christopher French, *Operations Manager*

Steve Ross, *Project Manager*

Doug May, *Project Superintendent*

Mike Wilhelm, *Masonry Contract Manager*

Scott Hesler, *Project Engineer*

Brian Tomcik, *Project Engineer*

Geiger & Peters, *Steel Fabricator*

Jim Calzoni, *President*

Evans Limestone, *Limestone Supplier*

Steve Evans, *President*

Frank Ira, *Project Manager*

Blakley Corporation, *Aluminum Window Contractor*

Jim Burton, *Project Manager*

Mansfield Stone, *Sandstone Supplier*

Trotter Construction, *Excavation Contractor*

Becker Landscaping, *Landscape Contractor*

Santarossa Mosaic & Tile, *Terrazzo Flooring Contractor*

Maltbie & Associates, *Permanent Exhibits Contractor*

Milgo Industrial, *INDIANA Obelisk Fabricator*

Landmark Clocks International, *Indiana Steam Clock Designer/Fabricator*

BOOK TEAM

Susan Williams, *Indiana State Office Building Commission*

Tony Nickoloff, *Indiana State Museum*

William Browne, Jr., *Ratio Architects*

Larry George, *Ratio Architects*

Richard Hunt, *Emmis Books*

Dana Boll, *Emmis Books*

Lloyd Brooks, *Thrive³*

Sarah Branham, *Thrive³*

Steve Mannheimer, *Author*

INDIANA STATE OFFICE BUILDING COMMISSION

Governor Frank O'Bannon, *Chair*

Lt. Governor Joe Kernan, *Vice Chair*

Betty Cockrum, *Secretary*

Tim Berry, Treasurer of the State, *Treasurer*

Members

Connie Nass, *Auditor of the State*

Glenn Lawrence, *Commissioner of the Department of Administration*

Eleanor Bookwalter

Brad Chamber

Myron Frasier

James Trotter

Henry Camferdan

Kenneth DeLap

Kipper Tew

Susan Williams, *Executive Director*

Robert Wilson, *Deputy Director*